The Sales Development Framework

How to Build and Scale a Highly Productive Sales Development Program

David Dulany

Kyle Vamvouris

978-1-7367689-0-7 (print)
978-1-7367689-1-4 (e-book)

Tenbound
152 Alexander Ave, Daly City, CA 94014

Visit us on the web:
https://www.tenbound.com/

tenbound

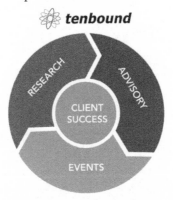

To my wife Katherine, who's indefatigable love and
support has made it possible for me
to live my dreams and find true happiness in my life.
I love you so much.

To my parents Ken and Joan Dulany
who gave me the love and support which enabled
me to enjoy a blessed and amazing life.

To all the professionals out there who
do their best every day to achieve their goals and
help others succeed, this book is for you.

— David

To my supportive wife Karlie
and our two kids Delphi and Dax.
Never let "reality"
convince you to limit your potential.

— Kyle

TABLE OF CONTENTS

ACKNOWLEDGEMENTS

Thank you to Francine Brevetti,
Sue Caulfield, Daniel Rose, Hannah Sullivan, Ben Hopfer, Vivian Chan,
Kristina Cayabyab, Katherine Dulany, and the whole Tenbound
and Vouris teams for their hard work helping put this book together.
A monumental effort.

For all our Sales Development mentors over the years,
too many to count, especially Ralph Barsi, Matt Amundson,
Liz Cain, Jake Dunlap, Doug Hall, Trish Bertuzzi, Scott Sinatra,
Pat Shah, Ryan Reisert, Sally Duby, Lars Nilsson, Max Altschuler,
Manny Medina, Mark Kosoglow, John Barrows, Carrie Simpson,
Kyle Porter, Henry Schuck, Craig "The Funnelholic" Rosenberg,
Andrea Waltz, Jeffrey Borovitz, Kyle Morris, Anton Lenke,
Bryan Elsesser, Scott Albro, Jacco van der Kooji,
Darryl "Uncle D" Praill, Sahil Mansuri,
and many more.

FOREWORD

"Every system is perfectly designed to get the results it gets."

—W. Edwards Deming

Building and scaling a Sales Development organization is not rocket science. There are, however, many parallels. There's the fuel, for example, that powers a rocket, and the physics involved to gauge velocity, trajectory, and altitude. And there are resources needed to ensure a proper lift-off, orbit, and landing—all of which are managed and monitored from mission control.

The two-fold objective of Sales Development teams is to contribute to their company's revenue pipeline and people pipeline. Contributions that are viable and repeatable are a must. If proper systems and processes are not put in place, though, to ensure a strong pipeline is created, then revenue and culture are compromised—the rocket does not complete its mission.

Leaders, this book is your flight plan. David and Kyle will educate and guide you on the mechanics of successful Sales Development functions. They will clarify and validate the best practices required to sustain positive outcomes. They will light a path forward and show you what to consider first, second, third, and so on. But the book won't make an impact unless you do something with its lessons.

Reps, this book describes what great looks like. It will influence how you show up, deliver strong results, serve others, and shape your career path. You'll also have an inside view of what keeps leaders up at night - from planning the work to working the plan. Applying what you learn from this book will instantly level up your game. The answers you seek are right here.

Similar to world class space programs, the Sales Development industry will continue to evolve: the question is whether you'll pioneer the effort or observe it. Future generations of Sales Development professionals are relying on you to lead by example, regardless of your role. And those who've gone before you expect you to raise the bar.

Create - or enhance - your business within the business. Use principles and examples from this book to model proven systems that yield proven results. When your Sales Development organization hums, it produces a high-quality revenue and people pipeline that catapults your company and customers into the stratosphere.

Light the fuse!

Ralph Barsi,
Sales Development Leader

"If your actions inspire others to dream more, learn more, do more and become more, you are a leader."

—President John Quincy Adams

INTRODUCTION

In this book, we lay out a proven approach detailing how to start, manage and accelerate your Sales Development program, whether you're a seasoned executive who needs to jumpstart a existing program, a mid-level manager is running your program on the daily basis, or an aspiring Team Leader or Sales Development Rep (SDR), who wants to move into management. This book can help you develop a course for success, in your company, your team, and your career.

The growth of Sales Development as a skill and niche in the past 10 years has been phenomenal. The Sales Development industry has exploded over the past 10 years and the volume of people, tools, and services involved in this industry continues to grow each year. Entirely new software categories have emerged to support this growth and some estimates have over 700k SDRs in the USA alone.

Primarily, in Software as a Service (SaaS) companies, Sales Development is finally seen as a strategic advantage to gain new customers and ensure high-quality pipeline and revenue.

The massive efforts required to gain a customer and sign them up for a service or subscription take time, money, and focus. The Sales Development team was created to apply that focus as a key business driver.

With the advent of the Predictable Revenue[i] model by Aaron Ross, many SaaS companies attempted to replicate the success of salesforce.com by starting their own Sales Development teams.

However, they quickly realized that Sales Development is a specialty that few understand. Without a roadmap or blueprint, many teams flounder. Still today, companies struggle to get their Sales Development programs right. Sales Development

---

i   Aaron Ross and Marylou Tyler, *Predictable-Revenue: Turn Your Business into a Sales Machine with the $100 Million Best Practices of Salesforce.com,* np.

Representatives (SDRs) burn out, Sales Development Leaders turn over, Account Executives (AEs) lack appointments, and the sales pipeline suffers[ii].

Maybe you are just starting out in your Sales Development management journey and need to know where to begin. Maybe you've inherited a team and you need to turn it around quickly. Maybe you're somewhere in between.

You may be asking: *Should we hire an SDR at all? Should we hire a full cycle sales rep first? Should we just outsource this whole department?* These and other questions keep founders, marketing, and sales leaders up at night.

There is no right answer or silver bullet, just educated hypotheses, strategy, execution, and ongoing course corrections. However, the fact remains, companies need new sales appointments, pipeline, and revenue now more than ever.

> ### *Now we realize that Sales Development is a specialty and it is a difficult one to master.*

We even struggle to figure out to whom Sales Development should report, whether to sales, marketing, or revenue operations.

The Sales Development Leader position has become a revolving door. Often, high-performing SDRs are promoted and quickly find out they don't have the skills or resources to execute their new job requirements successfully.

Account Executives are sometimes assigned to the Sales Development Leader role because of their expertise in selling; however, they quickly find out that Sales Development leadership is completely different from the individual contributor role and requires a different skill set.

At other times, Sales Operations professionals are put in charge of Sales Development because of their excellence in putting together the requisite systems, but they may not have the experience to deal with the people issues involved.

There has been a lack of focus on what it takes to create an excellent Sales Development program. The department tends to become a "hot potato" that after a while nobody really wants to step up and lead.

We wrote this book for someone new to Sales Development leadership, someone who wants to run a team, or someone who needs to understand how to get their pipeline cranking as soon as possible.

---

ii Throughout this book, we use SDR as an acronym for people in the position responsible for doing outbound prospecting, inbound lead qualification, or both. Sales Development Leader is used for people running SDR teams, and AE for full-cycle Sales Reps.

This book is full of actionable insights you can use to accelerate your team's growth and your personal career success.

This is the book we wish we had 10 years ago.

THE TENBOUND
SALES DEVELOPMENT FRAMEWORK
IS HERE TO HELP

■ HERE IS THE TENBOUND WAY

This is our uniquely crafted management operating system, which we use as the basis for our Sales Development Leadership Training. We conduct this class both virtually and in cities around the world and have built up an impressive alumni association in the process. These alumni continue to use our framework every day to push their programs forward.

The Tenbound Way explores each aspect of Sales Development leadership as an upward spiral of productivity. It's a manual you can use consistently moving forward. The system builds on itself and, as the success of your program grows, so does your reputation. Your reputation then leads to better opportunities where you will have more resources. Consequently, you will be able to execute on your vision and implement the process again, only bigger each time.

Our system also gives you a way to diagnose issues with your Sales Development program. For example, if you are a marketing executive who was just given the responsibility for your Sales Development pipeline, you may use the system to look at the program holistically. Are there gaps in the culture (or is it even defined?), the leadership, the analytics, or the recruiting process? Now that the problem is identified, what can be done to address it?

Once you have identified which part or parts of your program are deficient, you can rectify them by addressing one of three things: **people**, **processes,** or **technology.**

Some programs have enough technology, and even though those tools are great, success comes down to processes that are in place and, of course, to people.

We break the sections out in to a step-by-step format that creates a forward cycle of success:

THE TENBOUND SALES DEVELOPMENT MANAGEMENT OPERATING SYSTEM

THE TENBOUND SALES DEVELOPMENT MANAGEMENT OPERATING SYSTEM SECTIONS:

- ✓ *Culture*
- ✓ *Leadership*
- ✓ *Hiring*
- ✓ *Training*
- ✓ *Coaching*
- ✓ *Analysis*
- ✓ *Results*
- ✓ *Reputation*

CULTURE

In the culture section, we start at the beginning, laying a strong foundation for your goals, expectations, and within the mission of the Sales Development program, the importance of writing this down, iterating, and sharing it with the team.

LEADERSHIP

Gaining a good understanding of the difference between leadership and management is crucial. Not knowing the difference between the two is a weakness in Sales Development Leaders, sometimes creating a phenomenon known as the "**Dashboard Cowboy**."

HIRING

Once you have established a strong culture and you understand the importance of leadership as well as its difference from management, we move into using your culture statement to define your ideal team member and how to go about recruiting to find diverse top talent and to make sure you have a team of A-players.

TRAINING

After team development, we address how to create a world class training plan, one that will ensure that everyone on the team has all the knowledge, skills, and abilities to execute successfully, both on the job and in their future careers.

COACHING

Along with training, we dive into coaching and will help you understand the difference between the two. We discuss why the most important part of the job is coaching a team on a daily basis and why that will improve their skills incrementally.

ANALYSIS

Now that the team is in place, with regular training and coaching, we should start to see some results. From these results we are able to analyze how we set ongoing goals for the team, how we monitor conversion rates for their activities, how do we continuously iterate using the theory of constraints, and how we work with our company database to ensure that reps have enough people to call the people, that those people are prioritized and they're being constantly rotated, based on their changing status.

RESULTS

What are the results that were obtained from the program? How do we conduct A/B testing from those results and implement that concept of Kaizen[iii], or continuous improvement of Lean methodology[iv].

REPUTATION

Finally we discuss reputation, both yours and your team's and its perception within your company and the greater industry at large. We explain where to take all the great work you've done from running a high-performance Sales Development team and leveraging it into a successful career in Sales Development Leadership or other parts of the organization.

THE STRUCTURE OF THIS BOOK

You can use this workbook to develop your own world-class program. Each chapter begins with a brief overview of the topic within the operating system to be covered.

We recommend addressing each chapter sequentially as they build upon each other. Each chapter will end with a bullet-point summary of the main concepts.

By the end of this book, you will have a solid game plan that you can implement immediately to develop your Sales Development program.

With that page full of notes, you will have your strategy for the next three to six months to take your program to the next level. We have all read books where you find some useful information and have a good time reading it, but, at the end of the day, you stick it on your shelf and never think about it again.

---

iii Kaizen is a Japanese term meaning "change for the better" or "continuous improvement." It is a Japanese business philosophy regarding the processes that continuously improve operations and involve all employees. Kaizen sees improvement in productivity as a gradual and methodical process. The concept of Kaizen encompasses a wide range of ideas. It involves making the work environment more efficient and effective by creating a team atmosphere, improving everyday procedures, ensuring employee engagement, and making a job more fulfilling, less tiring, and safer. *https://www.investopedia.com/terms/k/kaizen.asp*

iv The Philosophy of Lean is the pursuit of performance (in terms of productivity, quality, lead times and costs) through continuous improvement and waste elimination, in order to satisfy the customer. For simplicity, the Lean method provides high quality work with minimal money, resources and time. The aim is to optimize the performance of processes by using the methods, techniques and practices already available in the company. What is Lean Methodology? Principles and Process of Lean Methodology, *http://www.businessstudynotes.com*

We are excited to put over 10 years of research, analysis and development down on paper to give you a guidebook and framework for creating your own amazing Sales Development program.

As you implement the changes suggested and start to turn around your own Sales Development program, keep in touch with us by following Tenbound and Vouris on LinkedIn, Facebook, and Twitter. Leave us a comment to let us know how things are working or where you need additional advice.

In this book we are going to show you how to build a strong Sales Development culture, one that will lead your team to great success. In fact, the
Tenbound Sales Development Management Operating System
will give you the tools you need for that success.

SALES DEVELOPMENT SELF ASSESSMENT

Whether you're starting your Sales Development program or already running it, assessing your current effectiveness in each area is essential.

RATE YOUR EFFECTIVENESS FOR EACH
ITEM WITH A <u>YES</u> OR <u>NO</u>

1. I have articulated the Sales Development Team culture.

2. I have shared our Culture Statement with our team and received their buy-in.

3. My leadership style, hiring practices and coaching techniques are imbued with our cultural values.

4. In my leadership style, I build up our team with encouragement, frequent coaching, and positive attitude.

5. The team sees me working alongside them, demonstrating the behavior I wish them to emulate.

6. I have created an Ideal Candidate Profile which includes all the personal and intellectual qualities we search for in candidates to create positive results.

7. Our search for candidates with a growth mindset is facilitated by the exercises we expect our candidates to complete during our interview process.

8. Our Sales Development Playbook is a complete resource for all the requirements new hires need to be productive.

9. We have instituted regular coaching sessions that provide constructive feedback, the opportunity for our team to practice skills, and to field questions.

10. We bring in outside trainers when specialized knowledge is required.

11. Our SDRs are productive, industrious, creative, and accountable.

12. We have calculated the number of calls and appointments we need to achieve results and have shared this information with our team.

13. We measure the quality of our team's calls and their ability to engage the prospect.

14. We encourage our SDRs to enhance their skills by engaging their colleagues, forming a network of friendly relationships.

HOW OFTEN DID YOU ANSWER YES?

10–14 times?
You're on track for great results.

3–9 times?
Dig in to all the chapters.

0–3 times?
Absorb this book and put it into practice today.

CULTURE

Culture Eats Strategy for Breakfast

Peter Drucker[i]

■ CULTURE? YES, THAT'S WHERE WE NEED TO START

If you think of any truly successful organization, they all have one thing in common—a strong culture. This is where we will start in creating your Sales Development program.

You can have the best strategy, the highest performing team, and the best possible products, but if your culture is toxic, your program will struggle.

The culture you create determines the people you hire, the processes you develop, and the technology infrastructure you put into practice. As a leader you are in control of the culture you want to establish within your program.

Culture is defined as the beliefs, customs, arts, etc. of a society, or group in a particular place or during a particular time. Every society has its own beliefs that are so deeply ingrained in the people of that society that they become the norm.[ii]

---

i   Management Consultant Peter Drucker (1909–2005) was called *the man who invented management* by Business Week magazine. His publications include *The Effective Executive*, *The Coming of the New Organization*, and *Management Challenges for the 21st Century*, to name a few.

ii   Taken from the Merriam-Webster definition of Culture, *https://www.merriam-webster.com/dictionary/culture*

*If culture is important for the entire company,
why should Sales Development think more about culture?*

Your company has a way of thinking, behaving, and working that spans all employees and departments and also affects your Sales Development program. However, as a Sales Development Leader, you need to establish your culture as well within your team. As a Sales Development Leader, your core competency must be to create and drive a strong culture, with well-established beliefs, customs, and values for your team.

■ WHAT YOUR CULTURE REFLECTS

A strong culture within your team is established by and will reflect:

- ✓ The leadership style you bring
- ✓ The hiring practices you employ
- ✓ The training and coaching you conduct
- ✓ The analysis you impart
- ✓ The results you achieve

All of the above are responsible for building the success and reputation of your Sales Development program. In addition to your reputation within the company, the culture you create will boost your reputation in the marketplace.

Culture is incredibly important. In fact, it is so important that the CEO and other executives in your company think about it a lot. So, why should you, as a Sales Development Leader, bother developing your own team culture?

IT'S SIMPLE.

Your team's culture is your program.

CULTURE AND COMMITMENT
CREATING YOUR IDEAL TEAM

■ WHAT KIND OF SALES DEVELOPMENT CULTURE DO YOU WANT TO CREATE?

Here are exercises to help you decide what culture you would like to create for your team.

EXERCISE 1:

WRITE DOWN YOUR ANSWERS TO THE FOLLOWING QUESTIONS.

1. What beliefs are important for you and your team to have?
2. If someone were to ask one of your SDRs *"What is your SDR program like?"*, how would you like them to respond?
3. What personal values do you feel are the most important for your team?
4. What are some attributes of a successful team culture?

By answering the previous questions, you should have some context to determine the type of culture you are striving to create.

EXERCISE 2:

HONE IN ON YOUR IDEAL CULTURE

Make a list of the attributes you would like to see in your Sales Development team. This list can consist of some of your answers to the questions in the previous exercise or new ideas inspired by those answers.

HAVING TROUBLE LISTING THOSE ATTRIBUTES?
TRY FILLING IN THE BLANK:

"Our Sales Development team is _____."

It is helpful when making this list that you ask your team members for their input. Try to keep the list to 4 or 5 items that will be easy to remember and will resonate with your team. Describe each with a sentence or two.

HERE'S AN EXAMPLE.

TEAMWORK: We work together to turn our goals into reality.

RESPECT: We respect all members of our team and company, even if we disagree with their ideas.

ENTHUSIASM: We are enthusiastic about what we do and it shows in our daily activity.

DISCIPLINE: We are disciplined and when we commit to something, we follow through.

Organize an offsite or Zoom session with your team to create this list of ideal attributes. Getting your team involved in the process of creating the culture is a great way to get them excited and help them commit to your newly defined or redefined culture.

■ DEFINING YOUR IDEAL TEAM MEMBER

Now that you have a better understanding of the culture you are creating, it's time to discuss the types of people who will thrive in that environment. Having a clear vision of the type of people you will hire will help you through the interview process. The outline of your ideal team member will also help you by giving you a framework to follow to ensure that the people you interview will fit into the culture you are creating.

WHERE TO START:

PAST COWORKERS AND TEAM MEMBERS

The first place to start when developing an outline of your ideal team member is to look at your past coworkers and team members.

Ask yourself this question:

*If I were starting a company, who is
the first person I would hire?*

Why would I hire them? What characteristics do they possess that would make them a valuable member of the team?

Write down the characteristics of everyone you thought of. It could include attributes like this:

✓ Honest

✓ Hard working

✓ Reliable

✓ Creative

✓ Fun

✓ Smart

✓ Personable

These characteristics should come together to paint a clear picture of your ideal team member.

YOUR COMMITMENT AS A LEADER

YOUR LEADERSHIP ASSESSMENT

How do you view yourself as a leader? If a member of your team is asked by a friend *How is [your name] as a leader?*, how do you think they will respond? Will they say *She's a lot of fun* or *He doesn't micromanage, so that's good.*? Alternatively, will they say *"She is so inspiring. I love how she runs the department."* or *"He's great. He always has our back and always pushes us to be better."*?

LEARNING TO LEAD

Being a great leader is a learned skill. Here's an exercise that you can do to help you shape your identity as a leader.

1. What are your values as a leader?
2. What kind of leadership style do you want to represent?
3. How do you define culture?
4. How do you imagine people in the future describing your program?
5. What does your vision of a great manager do daily?

Once your list is complete, reflect on how they align with your current performance as a leader and the culture you will create. Do you embody what you wrote down?

COMMITMENT TO LEADERSHIP

Commit to being the leader your list reflects.

Commit to being the best leader that you can be. Commit to living up to the standard that YOU set for yourself.

■ CREATING YOUR TEAM STATEMENT

The three exercises we just went through were to determine what culture you would like to create, who your ideal team member is, and your own commitment as a leader. These exercises are great for giving yourself clarity, but what about the rest of your team? What about the new employees you hire?

Your next step is to create statements that represent all components of your team, using the results of the three exercises.

THE CULTURE STATEMENT

A culture statement describes your vision for the future of your SDR program. This requires a thoughtful approach and starts with a strong list of team goals. Once you have that list, you can apply the attributes from the culture exercise to create your culture statement.

GOALS:

When you write your culture statement, you should start each unique point with "We believe…" or "Our team is…"

Your culture statement will include your vision, derived from the attributes you selected in the culture exercise, as well as the goals you just wrote down.

HERE'S AN EXAMPLE:

Our team is passionate about providing our customers with solutions to complex business problems. We are honest, productive, and we value of the success of the team over the individual. We work together and make amazing things happen.

Now, write down your own and once you complete it:

✓ Review it with your team

✓ Post it around your office or virtually

✓ Make it a screensaver

✓ Create posters

Put this message everywhere. Make it clear that these are the values that are important and that they are the ones that we will stick to as we build every part of the program.

THE IDEAL TEAM MEMBER STATEMENT

You've finished the culture statement. Now, let's do something similar with the ideal team member statement. The purpose of this statement is for you to have something that helps you visualize the type of team members you're looking to hire. In the interview process, it can sometimes be tempting to hire an individual who does not really align with your team's values. Having a strong ideal team member statement means you can remind yourself of the type of team you have committed to creating.

> *"It's expensive to hire the wrong people. If they leave it's expensive. If they stay it's expensive."*
>
> — Nathan Mellor,
> *Sleeping Giants: Authentic Stories
> and Insights for Building a Life That Matters*

Just as in the Culture Statement, you should start each point with "*The ideal member of this team is…*" or "*Our ideal team member…*" The remainder of each statement should be inspired by the diversity and characteristics that you wrote to describe your ideal team member.

HERE'S AN EXAMPLE:

Our ideal team member holds themselves to a higher standard than others do. They act with integrity and pull others up when they are down. They listen with focus, speak with precision, and genuinely care for the people they encounter.

Now, write your own ideal team member statement … with a pen and paper, of course (we should not have to keep reminding you to do this.).

THE LEADERSHIP COMMITMENT STATEMENT

The final statement you need to write is your statement of commitment as a leader. This is the easiest part to skip because if you're reading this book, let's face it, you are committed.

The reason why we require you to write this statement is because you will use it throughout your time as an Sales Development Leader. You are committed now, which is great. What about in 3 months from now? What about a year from now? Will you still be committed after 3 months of your team missing quota? Are you going to be able to stay committed when your top performing SDR quits? The purpose of your commitment as a leader statement is to have a written record of your commitment which will help hold you accountable.

Just as in the previous statements, start each point off with "As a leader I commit to…" followed by some of your answers from the exercise you completed earlier in this chapter. At minimum you must cover your values as a leader, the culture you are trying to foster, and what a great manager does daily.

HERE'S AN EXAMPLE.

"As a leader I commit to putting my team before myself. Because of this commitment I will put more effort into helping the individuals on my team than I do in making myself look good. I commit to creating a culture of encouragement, tough love, and consistent feedback. I am a leader who never misses a meeting with my team members, always listens before responding, and always pushes to be better every day."

Now that you understand the structure, take the time and write your own commitment as a leader statement. Make sure you are writing down things you will actually follow through on.

THE ONE-PAGE SUMMARY

The One-Page Summary is an overview of all the statements that you wrote

HERE'S THE FORMAT.

✓ Culture Statement

✓ Ideal Team Member Statement

✓ Commitment as a Leader Statement

✓ Objectives and Key Results for Your Team for the Next 90 Days

Here is what it would look like with our examples from above. Remember, one page, no more.

EXAMPLE OF THE ONE-PAGE SUMMARY

CULTURE STATEMENT

Our team is passionate about providing our customers with solutions to complex business problems. We are honest, productive, and we value the success of the team over the individual. We work together and make amazing things happen.

IDEAL TEAM MEMBER STATEMENT

Our ideal team member holds themselves to a higher standard that others do. They behave with integrity and pull others up when they are down. They listen with focus, speak with precision, and genuinely care for the people they encounter.

COMMITMENT AS A LEADER STATEMENT

As a leader I commit to putting my team before myself. Because of this commitment I put more effort into helping the individuals on my team than I do making myself look good. I commit to creating a culture of positive encouragement, tough love, and consistent feedback. I am a leader who never misses a meeting with my team members, always listens before responding, and always pushes to be better every day.

OBJECTIVES AND KEY RESULTS

✓ 100% average quota attainment

✓ 80% of team averaging 90% of quota and above

✓ New hires meet all ramp expectations

✓ Team building and motivation plan

✓ Conduct 3 after work team bonding meetups

✓ 1 team offsite

✓ Never miss a 1:1 with a team member

SUMMARIZE AND REVIEW YOUR SUMMARY

Now, take some time and write your own one-page summary. This is for you, so make sure you put in your honest objectives and motivation plan. This is important because you will review it every 90 days and evaluate your progress. Add a 90-day reminder in your calendar to ensure that you make time for this very important follow-up.

Each time you review, you should highlight all the things you've achieved. If you've achieved all the things you wrote down…*and this is the fun part*—reward yourself. You are the leader of the team. You take responsibility for the success and failure of the team. Do not publicly pat yourself on the back but do treat yourself to a nice dinner or a day trip to a favorite place.

You will not always accomplish everything on your one-page summary. This is one of the reasons a regular review is absolutely essential. Carefully review the objectives you did not meet.

ARE THEY TOO AGGRESSIVE?

If a goal is too aggressive, adjust it.

DID YOU PRIORITIZE GOALS CORRECTLY?

If priorities need realignment, realign.

This is YOUR one-page summary. You set the rules.

---

*Remember… Never make objectives too easy for yourself.
Always hold yourself to a high standard.*

If there is an objective that you did not achieve for a reason other than being too aggressive, keep it. Take note of why you did not achieve that objective and commit to making it a priority for the next 90 days.

The one-page summary is intended to help you hold yourself accountable. Reviewing it every 90 days and holding yourself accountable to what it says will result in improved results. Keep this in mind and treat the creation of the one-page summary as sacred.

THE 3 MAJOR TENANTS OF A STRONG SALES DEVELOPMENT CULTURE

Having a strong Sales Development culture requires you to be passionate about building a world class Sales Development team. The very fact that you are reading this book tells me that you are.

PRIORITIZATION

This is the first step in building a world class SDR team. What should be the main focuses for team creation? In our opinion, it comes down to three main tenants:

1. People

2. Process

3. Technology

◼ PEOPLE

The people on your team are your number one priority. You need to respect them, to treat them better than yourself, because people are paramount to team success. Your guidance helps each individual reach the sales potential required to reach every goal.

Remember...Without them you don't have a job.

PEOPLE VALUATION—PRIMARY FACTORS FOR BUILDING YOUR TEAM

RECRUITING

The people you hire can make or break your entire team. That might surprise you since the SDR role is very individualized. Can one person making calls, sending emails, and scheduling meetings to hit their quota really destroy the entire team's success?.

Even though the daily workflow of an SDR is individual, the role is extremely team oriented. Team success relies on every team member's contribution. It is imperative that you hire the right people—individuals who understand the importance of their contribution to a team.

Sales is challenging People who do challenging jobs tend to have strong comradery and that synergism creates team success,[iii]

TRAINING

In our experience, the best leaders prioritize training.

Having an effective training program not only improves the performance of your team, it shows them you care about their success and that you want them to grow, no only as team members, but also in their career paths.

The worst feeling a SDR can have is that they are on their own. They get rejected every day and, with no mechanism in place to improve their performance, they can fail. Show the people who work for you that you value them. Prioritize their training to help them successfully deal with every sales challenge and situation.

You know what they say about doing the same thing repeatedly and expecting different results?

We are what we repeatedly do.

Aristotle

PERFORMANCE MANAGEMENT

This is the difference between a poor leader and great one. Managing situations where an SDR is not meeting expectations is the third way you value your people. How do you deal with expectations when your entire team is missing the mark? How you handle this is the difference between bad and good leadership.

---

iii   Synergy is the interaction or cooperation of two or more organizations, substances, or other agents to produce a combined effect greater than the sum of their separate effects, Lexico (the Oxford English Dictionary), *https://www.lexico.com/en/definition/synergy*

> *A bad leader blames their people when performance slips.*
> *A great leader takes responsibility for their performance.*

PUT YOUR PEOPLE FIRST

That means that you take responsibility when things go wrong and you give them the glory when things go right.

Good or bad, you always point out opportunities for your SDRs to improve. The biggest mistake you can make as a leader is to see a behavior that is negatively impacting an individual or your team and not bringing it to their attention.

Your job is to challenge them to be better, even if it causes discomfort.

■ PROCESS

Later in this book, we will discuss process in detail, but we wanted to highlight their importance here. You can create the best culture and have the best tools, but without processes aiming all that energy in the right direction, you're toast.

You are the Sales Development Leader and your job is to build strong processes as well as identify and repair broken ones. As a process example, let's look at how your meetings are being booked today. What works really well about them? The easy answer is if a meeting is actually being generated, it has to be working well.

Let's flip the question

If a meeting is not being generated, what isn't working well? This is harder to answer, because the lack of results aren't always easy to explain.

As the Sales Development Leader you must be able to analyze a problem, identify the cause, and find a solution. You need to back your findings with actual data, because it is simply not good enough just to "know" the cause of a problem. Data gives you the proof you need and with the cause identified, you can take the necessary action to solve it.

Andrew Berger, Sales Development Leader, stresses: "SDR Leaders must be forward-thinking. You first need to work with your leadership to understand the company's core objectives. Once you know where the business wants to go, you can work backward from there. Start with an idea of realistic conversion rates, win rates, multiples, revenue, and profit. Set benchmarks for each metric. If things do not work as you suspected, systematically examine where there is a breakdown. What part of the funnel is not working? Is it the activity types? Is it something as simple as subject lines messaging? Is training insufficient? Are the personas off? Isolate what is not performing well and go fix that. Start at the beginning."[iv]

■ TECHNOLOGY

The final tenant of building a world class SDR culture is technology. Not every company can afford the most elaborate tech stack[v] available. You will always be working within a budget, however, there is no excuse for failing to leverage the full potential of the software you do have.

We see this all the time. A company spends a lot of money on software to make their SDRs more efficient…and it does. But, when asking the SDRs how they are using that software, we find out that they are still manually adding notes and customer information in the CRM (Customer Relationship Management) system.

As the leader, it is your job to know the workflow of your team inside and out. Knowing how your team is interacting with your technology will help you leverage the full functionality of those tools.

---

iv   Andrew Berger has built sales organizations at multiple companies.

v   The Sales Development Tool Stack is a set of software programs configured to support the work of SDRs and to integrate with Marketing, Operations, and Sales team' software programs in order to drive sales pipeline and revenue. The tool stack has become increasingly complex over the past few years as more tools are being created to support SDRs.

TAKEAWAYS

1. Write your Culture Statement

2. Write your Ideal Team Member Statement

3. Write your commitment as a Leader Statement

4. Create your one-page summary

5. Set a reminder to review your one-page summary every 90 days.

LEADERSHIP

Some people in management may feel that leadership is not a necessary factor in running a Sales Development program. They think that the Sales Development department is not important enough to warrant team leadership. You may hear something like this:

"It is just cold calling, isn't it? So, just tell them to cold call more."

We have a simple response when we hear this.

"Like any other organization, a big part of its success comes down to strong leadership."

Strong leadership is IMPERATIVE to building a consistent, top performing Sales Development team.

THE NEW SALES DEVELOPMENT LEADER

Make sure you have your culture statement documented and established. If not, go back to Chapter 1 and get it worked out. It is your foundation for success and the backbone of a high-performing Sales Development program.

LEADERSHIP STYLE

Once you have your culture defined and your team is onboard with the culture that you are creating, you will need to establish your leadership style and understand the difference between leadership and management.

■ LEADERSHIP VS. MANAGEMENT

The terms "leadership" and "management" are often intermixed, but we actually consider them two very different disciplines.

MANAGEMENT

Management is critical in planning and monitoring, making sure employees show up on time, get paid regularly, and do all the basic responsibilities they have been hired to do. It is very one dimensional; the manager is there to make sure tasks get done.

LEADERSHIP

Leadership is more dynamic. A leader defines a mission and creates a vision for the team. Leaders are there to empower people to do their best work, not just complete their basic responsibilities. A leader gives everything they have to their team in order to make them successful. Leading from the front[i], motivating team members, and pushing people to be better every day are all part of the day-to-day activities of a leader.

LEAD BY EXAMPLE

As a leader you must earn your team's trust, and they should believe that whatever you tell them to do is something you would do yourself. If you tell your team that they need to be in the office at 8am, you better be in earlier. If you want your team to do

---

i   As defined by *freedictionary.com*, to do the things or behave the way that one advises, dictates, or espouses; to take an active role in what you are urging and directing others to do.

a cold call blitz twice a day, you better be ready to throw on a headset and show them that you still got it and are willing to do it.

Great leaders don't hide behind spreadsheets, but they use that data to lead by example and rally their teams to do amazing things. This is the core difference between being a leader and a manager. This is an easy one to confuse; however, and something that needs to be established from the get-go.

You must be data driven and have expectations for your team. Activity levels, effectiveness, and work ethic are all important aspects of those expectations, but they are not nearly as important as the results that you deliver to the business. That's the metric that you, as the leader, are held accountable for.

THE DASHBOARD COWBOY

The Dashboard Cowboy term comes from the tech industry. It's a Sales Development Manager who sits behind his or her dashboard making sure everyone is on time, sitting at their desks making calls, and doing their jobs. What else are they doing to guarantee team success?

Don't get us wrong. You must be data driven and have a high work ethic for your team.

✔ *Work ethic* ✔ *Activity levels* ✔ *Effectiveness*

These are all important aspects of a Sales Development team. But, as a leader, the metrics you are held accountable for are the results you deliver to the business. Lead from the front, not the back.

DON'T BECOME A DASHBOARD COWBOY

■ A FRAMEWORK FOR GOOD LEADERSHIP

Great leaders are infectious and their team members follow them with confidence. This leads to more success as a team and results in empowering people to take ownership of their work, increasing quality.

The framework we've used for this book is the basic framework for being a good leader, not only a good manager.

We have broken down leadership into a simple acronym:

P.E.A.C.

✓ Prioritize

✓ Execute

✓ Attitude

✓ Competence

PRIORITIZE

This is the one that creates the most issues for a new leader.

New leaders are many times so focused on planning that they often struggle with prioritization. It's easy to get derailed by conflicting assignments when creating a plan on how your team is going to hit their numbers.

Let's say "Lisa" is a new Sales Development Leader who has created a plan that requires each SDR to make 50 calls and send 50 emails per day. It requires each SDR's conversion rate to increase by 1% over the next 3 months. Her plan to do this is by conducting regular training sessions three times a week.

On paper, this seems acceptable. If this were the only active task, I'm sure Lisa would knock it out of the park. The reality is that Lisa is going to be interrupted frequently. There will always be new projects, initiatives, and tasks that will fall on Lisa's lap and test her ability to prioritize.

LET ME ILLUSTRATE THIS WITH A WORK SCENARIO.

Lisa is one month into executing her plan. Her boss, the VP of Sales, says "We have an emergency board meeting in 4 days and I need you to put together some of your team's numbers for me to present."

Seems harmless, right?

It turns out that Lisa doesn't have the data to explain why their meeting to sales qualified meeting rate is 50%, down from 80% last quarter. The VP of sales knows that the board will ask about this number and tells Lisa to "figure it out." This is a complete manual process.

Not so harmless now, right?

Lisa has a decision to make. She can postpone the SDR training her team's needs to hit her planned 1% conversion rate increase. Alternatively, she could stick to the training schedule she planned and risk not being able to figure out why the sales qualified rate is down.

WHAT WOULD YOU DO?

Well, to be honest, it's a bit of a trick question. Most likely you would stick to your training plan and work a little extra over the next few days to get accurate data for the boss to present.

Scenarios like the one above happen all the time and you must be able to prioritize new objectives as they manifest.

A PROCESS FOR PRIORITIZATION

Here is a simple process you can follow to help you prioritize.

✓ Identify how long each of your tasks or projects will take

✓ Evaluate the impact of completing the task or project

✓ Prioritize the task or project that has the highest impact relative to how long the task or project will take

That process is great for planning priorities you know about, but what about when your boss needs something last minute?

ADJUSTMENTS TO YOUR PRIORITY SCHEDULE

In order to prioritize those last-minute tasks. you need to evaluate how important that task is.

When your boss asks you to add a task to your list, ask for the following information:

1. When do you need this completed?

2. What is the expected impact?

3. I am also working on X which I expect will result in Y. Would you consider this more important?

COMMUNICATION

Being open with your boss about what you are working on and getting agreement on the impact is a great way to keep yourself well organized and correctly prioritized. It also keeps your boss in the know of what you are working on. Your ability to prioritize will directly impact the success of your team so make sure you spend time prioritizing everything you do.

EXECUTE

Once you have your tasks prioritized you are now ready to execute. Execution is the most important skill you can develop in business and, we would even argue, in life. There is a common challenge that people face when it comes to executing.

FEAR OF FAILURE

The fear of failure will cripple you and your team's ability to accomplish what you need to do in order to succeed. Fortunately, this is easy to avoid. You may even think it's too simple.

Fully think through the situation.
Really? That's it?

YES AND HERE'S WHY.

In most cases, the worst possible scenario isn't as bad as it makes you feel. And, if the worst does happen, most likely, the only negative outcome is you needing to change the strategy. Strategy changes are not failures. If you take action and the strategy doesn't work, look at is as good. Now you know that you need to try something different.

"I have not failed. I've just found 10,000
ways that won't work."

—Thomas Edison.

When you are feeling overwhelmed or you think your lack the confidence in your ability to execute, ask yourself this series of questions.

1. What is the worst-case scenario?

2. If the worst-case scenario takes place, what would happen next?

3. How likely is this scenario?

Focus on execution and handle the outcomes as they come. Spending your mental and emotional energy fixating on the "what if's" will distract you.

> *Make a habit of asking yourself*
> *"what next" instead of "what if"*

ATTITUDE

Being a great leader takes time and is something you can't learn it overnight. The reason why is because leadership requires taking consistent action over long periods of time. That's how you earn the trust of your team and your bosses.

As we mentioned earlier, the core of being a great leader is the example you set for your team. You must not be afraid to get in the trenches. Remember, your team is watching you constantly to see how you "show up". They are mirroring every comment, reaction, and interaction you, as the leader, makes. Make sure your attitude is what you want your team to mimic and what you want the team to aspire to.

> *Leadership is you doing the right thing even if it's unpopular.*

You are being judged and you are setting the standard by which the team culture will be implemented.

FOR EXAMPLE:

Let's say one of your team culture aspects is **high-performance.** What are you doing to embody this aspect? If you are doing the bare minimum just to appear busy, obviously, you are not exemplifying that high performance attribute you expect from your team. You aren't living up to the cultural values that YOU set.

> *Trust us, your team will know.*

Maybe you are an excellent manager, ensuring that people are making phone calls and sitting at their desks at the right time. but you do not take ownership of their activity. You blame the team when they miss their number instead of yourself.

As a leader, you must take ownership of the results of the examples you set, the decisions you make, and the leadership style you have based on the culture that you have created for your team.

There are no excuses.

COMPETENCE

The concept of competence is a difficult one because there are two facets. The first is how well you are doing your job. That one's easy. The other, how do people perceive how well you are doing your job. Now, that's the hard one.

Let's tackle the first one, because it is the most "in your control."

HOW WELL ARE YOU DOING?

Being "*good at your job*" is ultimately tracked by the results you generate for the business. As the team leader, you are responsible for increasing its production. If your team is consistently successful, odds are you are competent.

Now, that was easy.

HOW DO OTHERS PERCEIVE HOW WELL YOU'RE DOING?

Let's tackle the hardest part of competence—how you are perceived by the people you work with. This includes your team, your peers, your boss, even your boss's boss. Everyone will be forming an opinion of you based on how well they think you are doing at your job. For all those individuals, you must behave in the way that you wish to be perceived.

This alone doesn't guarantee that other people's perception of you will be positive. but when your boss gives positive feedback on your performance, others tend to view you in a more positive light. This is one reason why it is so important to communicate effectively with the person or persons you report to. You should not stop at effective communication, plus it's better to over-communicate than say nothing at all. Leave nothing to the imagination because your boss may not know your efforts if you don't talk about them yourself.

Shocking? Yes, we know.

■ UPWARD COMMUNICATION

Below are a few things you should cover in every one-on-one with your boss.

✓ Activities you've done since your last meeting—calls, emails, etc.

✓ Meetings scheduled

✓ Updates on completed meetings

✓ Progress on your accounts

Any bad news or lack of progress must be followed by what you are going to do about it. Then, during your next discussion, you should share the results of the actions you've taken

> <u>Never</u> tell anyone about a problem without having a solution.
> <u>Never</u> propose a solution and neglect to take action on it.

■ LEADING BY EXAMPLE

Great leaders never tell their team to do something that they themselves wouldn't do.

Thinking of the best leader you know, what made them so great? Typically, the best leaders are the ones who have actually done the job. They know the ins and outs of the role and provide guidance on how to be effective.

Matt Amundson, CMO, shared a great anecdote on Tenbound's podcast, The Sales Development Podcast.

"As a leader, you will never have the respect and trust of the people who report to you unless they understand that you can perform the job. So, in order to prove that, I really set out early to, you know, I was an SDR myself, right? I made the phone calls. I sent the emails. I invested in our technology stack. I built out the process, so that by the time the first person had started, the quota that I was able to give them was one that I was achieving before I'd even hired somebody. The process that I laid out for them was one that I was already doing. And so, I built in an early level of trust with my first couple of hires, and they were brilliant. I mean, they were great and they totally bought into the process. They were super successful. My first three SDRs are currently account executives here at the business."

Being a great leader will allow you to shape your career and propel you to where you desire to be. leadership is challenging and the skill is always in demand. In a later chapter we will discuss the different directions that the sales development manager can go in his or her career path.

MOTIVATION—A STORY FROM THE TRENCHES

Kyle Vamvouris

I remember one situation during my startup experience that really stands out and illustrates the power of motivation. There was less than a week left in the month and my team was behind on their quota by a significant amount—i.e. it basically was not going to happen. Morale was down and despite my efforts to cheer up the team, they felt down on their luck. Then something special happened.

The entire company was packed into our small conference room for an "all hands" meeting. There wasn't enough space in the room and 10 people had to stand outside and cup their hands over their ears just to hear. I was one of those people.

My boss was giving his update and said: "As for the SDR team, they are not going to get close to hitting quota this month."

My jaw hit the floor. You never claim defeat before the final bell tolls.

I quickly said "hey." a little too loud as I squeezed passed my colleagues to get into the conference room. The entire company was staring at me and you could hear a pin drop.

I wasn't thinking, I was reacting.

"Don't count us out. Does it look like we will hit quota? No. Not even close. But what I can tell you is that if ANY team can do it, it's this one. Do NOT count us out."

The next day I pulled my team aside in the morning and addressed what happened the day before. We all agreed. We were going to make them eat their words.

What happened next was nothing short of amazing. I had never seen my team so fired up. They were cheering each other on, laughing together, and booking more meetings than they even thought possible.

Over the next four days, they broke their "most meetings booked in a day" record twice.

And when the final bell tolled, we were short by one meeting.

You would have thought we had beat our quota by 200%. They didn't care that we missed our team quota by one. They were ecstatic because when everyone in the company thought we couldn't get close, we did.

The next month was the biggest one we ever had.

After that experience, I started spending 10 minutes every morning with my team reminding them of why we are doing this. Pointing at our previous successes and pointing to the potential successes on the horizon. I never stopped motivating the team. I never stopped reminding them of what we accomplished and challenging them to repeat it.

■ ■ ■

A team is a group of individuals rallied around a specific objective. Unfortunately, daily work often has a way of causing the individual to lose sight of that objective. This is very prevalent in SDR teams because it comes with rejection, repetitive tasks, and variables outside of their control.

TAKEAWAYS

✓ Define and document your ideal leadership style.

✓ Define the leader you want to be known as

✓ Ensure you are leading by example at all times.

✓ Write down three specific actions you can take on a regular basis to live into that ideal.

HIRING

Now that the culture you want to create and your leadership style is documented, it is vital to get the right people in place to build your culture and execute your Sales Development strategy.

As Jim Collins puts it in his seminal work, *Good to Great: Why Some Companies Make the Leap...And Others Don't*[i], "...getting the right people on the bus in order to ensure you have a chance to hit your goals is your highest priority. Without the right people on your team, it becomes almost impossible to move forward."

Bill Gates, Steve Jobs, and Sir Richard Branson all emphasize the importance of hiring the right people to support your strategy. Winning requires a great team and a great team makes winning a lot more fun. We call this the upward positivity spiral[ii].

Not everyone you hire is going to be an "A" player, and that's fine. "B" players still have a place on a team and great leadership can drive "B" players to produce incredible results.

> *You absolutely need the best possible people*
> *you can find to support your strategy.*

Always hire carefully and implement a recruiting process that strives toward a diverse team of "A" players.

---

i   Jim Collins, *Good to Great: Why Some Companies Make the Leap and Others Don't*, HarperBusiness, 2001, np

ii   "Positive thinking and its power to self-generate an upward spiral is a concept from Barbara Fredrickson's Broaden-and-Build theory. This theory asserts that positive emotions broaden one's attention and cognition, and therefore initiates upward spirals of emotional and physical self-development.", All About the Upward Spiral Effect, Gloveworx, December 5, 2017, np

> ### <u>Never</u>, under any circumstances, hire an SDR just because you "need" someone to start right away.

Even if you have all the best processes, tools, technology, and the right strategy in place, having the wrong people on board will drive down your success or halt it entirely. Even worse, toxic people can take a high-performance team and stop it dead in its tracks.

Because you only want to hire the best, you have to cast a wide net and you (or someone on your team) must be continuously recruiting. The quality of the team will be a reflection of your abilities as a leader; therefore, it's in your best interest to consistently scout for new, top-tier talent.

■ HIGH-LEVEL HIRING STRATEGIES

When you begin the process of hiring SDRs, you first need to look at the go-to-market strategy [iii] of your company.

For example, will your team be responsible for following up with inbound or outbound leads? Perhaps they will be responsible for a hybrid of both. Maybe your team will be divided by industry vertical [iv] or be responsible for pursuing a limited number of target accounts in an account-based model [v].

The go-to-market strategy and team format will determine the type of candidate you bring on the team. You must know this before you start deciding on who to hire.

INBOUND VS OUTBOUND PROSPECTING

Here is an example of people who excel in inbound vs. outbound prospecting and the difference between the two.

---

iii   Go-to-market or a go-to-market strategy is how a company uses internal and external resources to deliver their brand to customers and subsequently achieve a competitive advantage.
iii   An industry vertical describes a group of companies that focus on a shared market area. Also called vertical markets, industry verticals almost any industry type.
iii   "Account-based marketing, also known as key account marketing, is a strategic approach to business marketing based on account awareness in which an organization considers and communicates with individual prospect or customer accounts as markets of one. Account-based marketing is typically employed in enterprise level sales organizations." Wikipedia, *https://en.wikipedia.org/wiki/Account-based_marketing*

THE INBOUND PROSPECTOR

When building an inbound team, you are looking for candidates that are more customer-service oriented. They should be thoughtful, helpful, friendly, and more empathetic to others.

THE OUTBOUND PROSPECTOR

When hiring outbound SDRs candidates must be extroverted, able to handle uncertainty, push through fear, and unfazed by rejection.

THE HYBRID PROSPECTOR

If doing both inbound and outbound, the candidate must be a well-rounded combination of the two.

As you can see, these personalities are very different. When going through the hiring process, if you are unable to determine what type the SDR candidate is, you may end up hiring the wrong person.

GROWTH

You should always look for team members who want to grow with your company. By hiring and training highly successful SDRs, you are laying the groundwork for their success and the success of the company as they rise through the organization. The future of the company can come from your team, if you build it right.

DEVELOPING THE IDEAL CANDIDATE PROFILE

Remember the Creating Your Ideal Team Member Statement from an earlier chapter? Well, this is where that will come in handy. Your Ideal Candidate profile is a document that outlines the type of candidate you are looking for. This will need to be a shared document so it's clear to everyone involved in the hiring process what type of candidate you're seeking.

Your Ideal Candidate Profile should include the three or four highest priority attributes of the candidates. What are the "must haves" they bring to the table in order to be considered for the position? What are the red flags or yellow alerts you want to watch out for to ensure you don't get the wrong people?

Thinking about your current, highest performing SDRs, what is it about them you would clone to create the perfect team member? Those characteristics are critical, so write them down so you have a target to follow.

Here are few things to look for in your ideal candidate profile regardless of whether they will be in an inbound or outbound role:

✓ Smart and open to learning

✓ A track record of success

✓ A growth mindset

✓ Goal orientation

✓ Great communication skills in writing, speaking, and listening

✓ Determined, organized and outgoing

> ### *Always identify the role your SDR hire is going to fill and then, hire for that role.*

To expand on the example we used earlier in this chapter, if you are hiring for an inbound SDR position, focus on finding the candidate with those attributes. The reason why we bring this up is because many companies create a stair-step career plan where people start at inbound and then get promoted to outbound and eventually to Account Executive.

> ### *Having a progression program is great, but starting that progression with inbound may not always be the best solution[vi].*

Giving inbound leads to your most junior SDRs is something we typically recommend avoiding. Inbound leads are the result of tremendous investments in brand, product, processes, and time. They are so valuable, they need to be handled with kid gloves by your most competent, experienced SDRs. In our ADHD world, gaining someone's attention long enough to perform an inbound action is an almost impossible task.

> ### *Treat these as gold.*

---

vi   The thought behind having a progression that starts with inbound is that some people believe inbound is an "easier job." However, we argue that inbound is a very important job that needs to be handled carefully. Inbound interest is expensive to produce and needs to be handled with extreme care.

It's harder to get an inbound SDR to switch gears and start making cold calls for the first time than it is to have an outbound SDR call on warmer leads.

PERSONALITY AND SDR TYPE

Also, as we've discussed, the personalities for the successful inbound SDR can be different than those of the outbound SDR and often we see these SDRs moving into marketing or customer service roles, as opposed to AEs. Outbound SDRs, on the other hand, tend to lean towards an AE position.

Knowing the possible career paths for the type of candidate you are looking for helps you create a clear Ideal Candidate Profile. Once you have your Ideal Candidate Profile written down for each role, it can be used by multiple people involved in the hiring decision to help find and hire the best possible candidates for the job.

SALES VS THE REST OF THE COMPANY

Sales Development is very different from other parts of a company because SDRs don't usually stay in that position for long before moving on to something else.

As an example, let's say you change companies. If you're running a marketing team you could, conceivably, bring three or four of the rock stars from your old marketing department with you to your new company because marketers typically stay marketers and remain loyal to good management. However, unlike other parts of the company, if you're leading a Sales Development team and you change jobs, you most likely won't be able to bring any SDRs with you, because rock star SDRs from your old company have already been promoted.

LONGEVITY AND THE SDR TEAM

If you are running a high turnover program that's very process-oriented, then high turnover is built into your company's DNA and can be justified financially. But if you want to keep people around for a long time, you're going to have to build your process accordingly, one that takes care of people and gives them the ability to find new opportunities within the company.

Regardless of your company's individual situation one thing is consistent—you will always need to be hiring.

■ THE CANDIDATE FUNNEL

This is considered a "top-down" approach to successful hiring. It is a multi-step process for finding the right candidates for hire. It's called a funnel, because a lot of candidates go in at the top, process through multiple steps before getting to the bottom where they may accept your offer of a position. Through the steps, candidates may drop out or may not be asked to continue. After traversing through the tunnel, you are left with a smaller pool of potential candidates.

THE TOP OF THE CANDIDATE FUNNEL—WHERE FINDING CANDIDATES STARTS

Here's how to create a huge candidate funnel at the top of the screening process.

- ✓ Attend events in your community that are geared toward Sales Development professionals
- ✓ Attend career fairs
- ✓ Contact candidates directly on Linkedin
- ✓ Join Meetups on Sales and Sales Development (or start them)
- ✓ Take the top Sales Development recruiters in your neighborhood out to lunch and make sure that your opportunity stays on their radar screen
- ✓ Get to know any Sales Boot Camps in your city. Make sure that they're aware of the opportunities that are available at your company

As you build a pipeline of candidates you will find that you are not the only company interested in hiring them. This is exactly why your personal brand matters.

■ HIRING AND YOUR PERSONAL BRAND AS A LEADER

It is important to work on your personal brand and consider your presence online. You want your personal brand to reflect how amazing it will be to be on your team. We will discuss this in more detail in Chapter 8: Reputation.

The reality is that we live in a social-media-connected world and potential candidates are looking for opportunities through those networks. These candidates will look at your company's website and your personal social media profile to see if this is the place where they want to work. This potentially drives inbound traffic and so, your personal brand can make the difference between an SDR deciding to accept your offer and not accepting your offer.

*Take a step back and give your "online self" an objective look.
What kind of leader are you?*

- ✓ Are you speaking at conferences?
- ✓ Are you posting how-to videos?
- ✓ Are you posting pictures of accomplishments of your team?
- ✓ Are you posting pictures of your team having fun outside of the office?

A strong leader uses social media to show leadership strength and to captivate "A" players to join in the success of their Sales Development group.

THE INTERVIEW PROCESS

We cannot stress this point enough—you must have a structured interview process that is both effective at identifying top level talent and quick to move candidates through the funnel.

Identification of top talent is first because you are looking for "A" players. Quick to move candidates through the funnel is second, because you don't want to miss out on "A" players because of a slow process.

RECRUITING STEPS

Let's take a deeper look at the recruiting process for building your dream team.

To find the right people for your team you will need a recruiting process laid out, organized, and documented. The outline below is what we use and recommend, but feel free to adjust it to fit your needs.

1. The pre-screening process

2. The pre-screening assessment

3. The phone screening process

4. Live exercise role-play

5. Live interviews

6. Internal discussions

7. Offer

THE RESUME PRESCREENING PROCESS

Prescreening is the first step in your hiring process. You will prescreen candidates to determine if you would like to speak with them to learn more about their background (the phone screen).

The benefit of the prescreening is that it will keep you from spending too much time on unqualified candidates. In addition, this process will prevent high quality candidates from getting lost in a pile of resumes, because you will be quickly scan through those resumes to identify qualified candidates.

Prescreening via resume review is quick because you will be looking for evidence of three to four characteristics. These characteristics are different for outbound, inbound and hybrid[vii] roles.

HERE ARE THREE SDR TRAITS THAT YOU CAN QUICKLY FIND WITHIN A RESUME.

1. HAVE THEY EVER SOLD ANYTHING?

When skimming through a candidate's resume search for evidence that they've sold something. If they have, that's great. If they provide their track record, even better.

---

vii   Hybrid is where an SDR has both inbound and outbound responsibilities.

Keep in mind, this might not be a traditional sales role. Keep a lookout for unconventional "sales experience" such as, Girl Scout cookies, Cutco knives, College Works Painting, etc. There are hundreds of sales opportunities that kids or teenagers can pick up without any background or any knowledge of sales. If a candidate does have sales experience, they are worth additional consideration.

2. HAVE THEY EVER DONE SOMETHING ON THEIR OWN INITIATIVE?

Maybe they started a small business or a hobby blog. Any sign of initiative is a great indicator that this person will be adaptable and function well in the "unknown."

If you are looking at a resume that indicates little initiative or few of the other traits you are looking for, you may want to pass.

3. DO THEY HAVE A GROWTH MINDSET?

If you spot continuous education or educational extracurricular activities on their resume, that's a good sign. It means they are continually looking for improvement… for growth.

COACHABILITY

It's hard to tell if someone is coachable just by reviewing their resume, which is why it is not included in the traits you should consider. You want coachable people on your SDR team because they often are the best at adapting to change and ramping up quickly. If an SDR is not coachable, they will get very frustrated when they face multiple weeks of failure. To compound that challenge, that SDR will probably not be able to implement your advice well.

HOW TO TELL IF SOMEONE IS COACHABLE

To tell if someone is coachable, ask about a time when they were struggling and received advice, then put it in practice to improve. Do they have a few ready answers? Ask what it was they did to improve when they did struggle. Did they seek guidance and then, followed the given suggestions? During the interview, ask them to perform an action, then give them some advice about that action and have them do it again. Did they implement your suggestions on the second try? Mark Roberge suggests this in his book "*The Sales Acceleration Formula: Using Data, Technology, and Inbound Selling to Go from $0 to $100 Million.*"

You can also practice a script with them and throw them on some live calls. In this scenario, you can make a list of old leads which have gone cold, and no one is interested in calling. Give the recruit a sales script and list of old leads to call. As Mark Roberge suggests, have them call through the list, talk to some prospects, and then recap their progress. Give them some advice, and then have them do more. See if they implemented the advice to check for coachability.

ATS[VIII] VS RESUME SKIMMING

Quickly skimming resumes looking for specific traits that indicate a good candidate will help you prioritize potential candidates for each position. We suggest doing this for all resumes, even if you have an applicant tracking system (ATS) that does this for you. We often find that high quality candidates can get lost in these systems before you ever see them. Make sure that you go through each resume yourself or with your recruiting partners if you have them. This way you are less likely to miss a diamond in the rough. Sales Development is about results. Look for candidates with a diverse background. All different experience levels, locations, and backgrounds can lead to success in Sales Development.

THE PHONE SCREEN

After you have pre-screened someone and are interested in learning more about them, it's time to schedule a phone screen.

Many organizations have the recruiter do an initial phone screen which saves the hiring manager a lot of time. At always keep in mind that the recruiter may have different goals than you. The recruiter might have dozens of open job positions that they must fill, ostensibly, with the "right candidate."

It is up to you if you would like to be involved in the first phone screen with the candidate. At a bare minimum you should have your own phone screen once the recruiter gives the green light.

YOUR IDEAL PHONE SCREEN

Keep your initial phone screens short and to the point. Also, keep in mind that each person you screen by phone is probably going directly to Glassdoor after talking with you and recording their experience. So, you want to make sure that it's a pleasant call for the candidate.

---

viii   An applicant tracking system is a software application that handles potential candidate recruitment.

During your phone screen have your ideal candidate profile in front of you. Use it to direct your questions for the candidate. Before the call, look through their resume again for their track record of success, and for whatever other aspects of your ideal candidate profile requires that they may have.

You do not have to spend the full scheduled time with the candidate. If you know within the first five minutes this person is not a good fit based on your ideal candidate profile, politely end the call. This is important, especially if you notice two or more "red flags." A red flag could be anything from poor past performance to having a negative personality.

During your phone screen, the candidate should be able to catch your attention quickly. This is important because if they are going to be an SDR and they will be expected to catch the attention of your prospects quickly. If they cannot sell themselves, someone they have known for a while, how are they going to sell your solution?

EXERCISES AND ROLE-PLAY

We are advocates of live exercises during the interview process. Unfortunately, many managers skip this because they fear it will consume time. Really, there's no reason to make it complicated and excessively drawn out.

We would argue that live exercises are to your advantage. Even a very simple exercise can give you a window into the candidate's strengths and their weaknesses, their communication style or lack of it. This will also help give you an idea of where they might need coaching, which allows you to plan better. Exercises are an effective way to screen out poor candidates.

WRITTEN AND VERBAL EXERCISES

There are the two main exercises we consider most valuable

1. TEST THEIR WRITING SKILLS

Have them send you a follow-up email summarizing the interview and explaining why they would like the work at your company. Have them outline the value they can bring to the company. Again, evaluate their ability to sell themselves.

THE "MEH[ix]" EXAMPLE

Dear Jake,

Thank you for the interview. I think I'm a good worker and your group is cool. I hope I didn't sound too acrimonious when I talked about that training at my old company. Yours seems pretty avant-garde. If you hire me I promise I won't be a boondogggler and I'm definitely not a dilettante. BTW...I would fit right in to your softball team, because I'm a pitcher. You said you needed one, right?

Hope to talk to you again, soon.

Bert

WHAT DOES THIS SHOW YOU ABOUT YOUR CANDIDATE'S WRITING SKILLS?

✓ Writing a lot but expressing little

✓ Not spellchecking

✓ Using words that sound pretentious

✓ Using an informal introduction

✓ Using slang

✓ Reiterating conversational points that do not reflect job capabilities.

2. TEST THEIR VERBAL SKILLS

Have them do a role play with someone on the team. Don't go easy on them either. Throw some objections in there and see how they do under pressure. You can also practice a script with them and throw them on some live calls.

After they complete the verbal exercise, give them some advice and let them give it another try. This helps you understand how well they implement improvement...how well they can be coached. If they do not do a good job taking your advice, it could be a sign that they are not open to feedback and are not willing/able to accept change.

---

ix   Writing that expresses a lack of interest or enthusiasm, uninspiring, unexceptional.

Accepting feedback, both good and bad,
is essential to success.

■ THE INTERVIEW

All the prescreening and phone screening has led to this—the actual interview.

The success you have as a company is directly tied to the people you hire.

We recommend you read a book on interviewing to get a holistic view of the skill. One such book is Joe Miller's, "*Great Sales People Aren't Born, They're Hired - The Secrets To Hiring Top Sales Professionals.*"

INTERVIEWING BASICS

The purpose of this section will be to cover the basics of interviewing and some common questions you can ask. In addition, we include a question in every interview that allows us to evaluate the candidate within the first 5 minutes.

INTERVIEW GOALS

There are two primary goals of an interview

1. Evaluating the candidate

2. Convincing them to work at your company

You must identify whether they are going to be a good fit for your team and convince them that your team is a good fit for them.

We recommend having a minimum of three people interview the candidate. One should be your boss, another, someone from your team and, of course, you. Having multiple perspectives helps because each person will have a different experience with the candidate. One person might have a specific concern that gets nullified by someone else's interaction with the candidate. Having multiple interviewers helps eliminate biases towards a specific candidate.

YOU, AS INTERVIEWER

When it's your turn to interview the candidate, you must consider this specific question—what do you need to identify in order to be excited about this particular candidate? If you don't know the answer to this question before you go into the interview, you may find it much harder to evaluate the traits you are looking for.

Also, and similar to the phone screen, you should be asking questions that align with your ideal candidate profile. We recommend asking questions about how the candidate has displayed those qualities in the past.

HERE ARE SOME EXAMPLE QUESTIONS.

- ✓ How do you handle rejection?
- ✓ Do you enjoy talking on the phone?
- ✓ What do you like about sales?
- ✓ Tell me about a time you faced a challenge. How did you deal with it, and what motivated you to keep going?"
- ✓ If I give you some feedback on changes to X, Y, and Z, would you use that feedback? Why or why not?"
- ✓ How do you go about learning new skills?
- ✓ What do you think will be the most common objections you'll hear during a call? How would you handle them?"
- ✓ Do you have any questions for me?"

THE CHET HOLMES TECHNIQUE[x]

This is not for the faint of heart: Have the job candidate call you. At the beginning of the interview ask an open-ended question. Have them answer, and then when done simply say *"I'm not hearing an A-Player"* and stop talking. Monitor their response, then again simply say *"I'm not hearing an A-Player"*. How do they handle it? Do they keep their composure, or fold? You are trying to tease out how flexible they are under stressful circumstances on the phone right now, before they learn from actually being on the phone with prospects. You may have just saved them and yourself months of agony.

---

x   Chet Holmes (1957 – 2012) was a top marketing executive, trainer, strategic consultant, and motivational expert for many of the Nation's Fortune 500 companies. Chet Holmes, *Hiring Sales Superstars*, YouTube, 09/22/2008.

When they are in an SDR role, they will be forced into this position on a daily basis. Each person that you bring on your team must master this kind of challenge. If they cannot handle it during the application, how are they going to handle it after you hire them? This is an attribute that is very difficult to train; it's inherent in a person's personality. Building a team of winners is hard but, if you have a team of winners, your life will be a lot easier down the road. You can instead assume your true role as a leader, mentor and coach.

KYLE'S INTERVIEW QUESTION

Kyle has a very good interview question that he swears by. It only works if you are the last person to interview the candidate. Here is the question.

"At this point you have interviewed with Person 1 and Person 2. After our conversation here I will sync up with them and discuss you as a candidate. I'm curious, from your perspective, what will they say they are most excited about you as a candidate and what do you think their biggest concerns will be?"

This question is so powerful because you get a window into their own self-awareness. You get to hear what they believe the other interviewers are excited/concerned about them. In addition, the candidate gets the opportunity to overcome those concerns. This question gives you so much insight into the candidate as a person, give it a try.

INTERNAL DISCUSSIONS

Remember again, this is your team. You are the person who is responsible for delivering solid results on a weekly, monthly and quarterly basis. Do not let other people determine who will be on your team. Certainly, solicit their input, and take it seriously, but at the end of the day, it's your call.

HOW CAN YOU GAIN FEEDBACK?

Ensure everyone on your interview team is on the same page in the process. Typically your interview team consists of your superior, someone in marketing or one of your team members. First, distribute your ideal candidate profile to each of the members. This ties straight back to your culture and strategy document. You know the culture you're trying to create on the team and the strategy you're putting in place. Make clear to the other people involved what you're looking for and what you're willing to accept.

This becomes especially difficult when your boss is involved. Many times, your boss will try to tell you whom to hire. Take their feedback and let them know you respect it but make your own decisions. If they won't approve the people you're sending, you need to understand and embrace your superior's requirements. If the candidates you are excited about continuously get rejected by your superior, you must sync up and make sure you understand their requirements. Your boss and others might start to lose respect for you if you're sending them unqualified candidates, from their perspective.

HERE IS HOW TO STREAMLINE THIS PROCESS

Set up a shared Google Doc with a 1 to 5 point drop-down menu for each of the top 5 to 10 attributes you're looking for. You can also give the interview committee the questions you want to ask the applicant and then ask the committee for feedback on the form. Aggregate the ratings and then you can correlate them back to successful SDRs in a few months. If someone on the interview group is late or doesn't turn in their forms, you can remove them from the interview group. You need engaged team players, delivering data, not just opinions.

Once your interview process has run and you have all your data and your manager has approved, it's time to make the offer. Before you do that, put a calendar reminder for six months in advance to go back and compare the data you compiled on the candidate during the interview process with the performance and attitude of the SDR since they've been on your team. How do they relate? Do you need to change the questions, change the culture statement, change the ideal candidate profile? What tweaks do you need to make to continue developing and iterating on your high-performance team?

No process is perfect right out of the box, so you must iterate it over time. The purpose of having this rating system is it makes the internal conversations much easier.

THE OFFER

When all the pieces are in place, it's time to make the offer. This is a happy time and a lot of fun, so enjoy it, but also be ready for a variety of responses. Best case, the prospective new team member could take the first offer, sign off and you're done.

Keep in mind though, they may come back for more money or better benefits. Or, they may come back and say they have other offers and they're evaluating each. The key for you as a manager is to not be surprised by any of the various requests; be ready with your responses for each. Below are the common points for negotiating an offer.

✓ Higher salary

✓ Higher commission

✓ Better benefits

✓ Relocation bonus

If they sign off, make sure you're ready to start your training program (see Chapter 5 on coaching) and you have all the dates and processes ready for the start date.

TAKE CHANCES

Hiring is tough and the decisions you make will be a reflection of you as a leader. Because of this fact it can be really challenging to "think outside the box" when making hiring decisions. We want this section to encourage you to take changes and use your gut when hiring.

In a perfect world, every candidate will have pros and cons that are easy to see and use in your decision making. Unfortunately, this world isn't perfect. Sometimes there are people who don't fit the mold. A great leader can spot these "diamonds in the rough" and shape them to be top performers.

If you are considering hiring a candidate that doesn't fit the profile of someone you would typically hire, don't write them off. Some of the best employees have unconventional backgrounds, but unbelievable work ethic and grit.

HERE'S AN EXAMPLE:

Kyle once met a young man who was looking for an SDR job but lacked a college degree. He kept facing rejection after rejection while simultaneously detailing cars to make enough money to pay rent. He was passionate about sales but no one would give him a shot. Kyle was not hiring at the time but helped him improve his resume and prepare for interviews. He ended up getting a job and being the top performer there, outworking everybody.

You see, that young man had something that they don't teach in school—unwavering drive. If you can build a team filled with people with that level of determination, you can accomplish anything. Take chances, use your gut, and seek out talent in unusual places.

TAKEAWAYS

✓ Decide on your high-level hiring strategy

✓ Refine your own personal brand as a leader

✓ Stick to an interview process

✓ Take chances and never be afraid to bet on a
person with drive

ONBOARDING AND TRAINING

The importance of onboarding[i] and ongoing training of SDRs cannot be understated. You interviewed multiple candidates, chose who you felt would be the best fit, and convinced them to join your team.

The candidate interviewed at multiple companies, received multiple offers, and decided that you and your company were the right fit for their career.

As the leader, onboarding and training are how you live up to the expectations you set during the interview process. Now is the time to make sure they start out on the right foot.

The number of stories we hear about companies that hire SDRs and leave them to "sink or swim" is mind-boggling. In fact, Gallup finds that "only 12% of employees strongly agree that their organization does a great job onboarding new employees[ii]."

Here are a few Onboarding Statistics.

✓ Great employee onboarding can improve employee retention by 82%[iii]

✓ 88% of organizations don't onboard well[iv]

✓ 58% of organizations say their onboarding program is focused on processes and paperwork[v]

✓ After onboarding, 20% of new hires usually don't recommend a company to a friend or relative[vi]

---

i "Onboarding, also known as organizational socialization, is management jargon first created in the 1970s that refers to the mechanism through which new employees acquire the necessary knowledge, skills, and behaviors in order to become effective organizational members and insiders." Wikipedia, *https://en.wikipedia.org/wiki/Onboarding*

ii Ben Wigert and Ryan Pendell, 7 Problems with Your Onboarding Program, Gallup, *https://www.gallup.com/workplace/247172/problems-onboarding-program.aspx*, March 1, 2019

iii Madeleine Laurano, Brandon Hall Group, The True Cost of a Bad Hire, August, 2015, p. 12

iv Gallup, State of the American Workplace, 2017, p. 36

v Sum Total, Talent Pulse, Onboarding Outcomes, 2016, p. 6-8

vi Digitate, Super CIO, What the CIO sees that other people don't, 2018

✓ great onboarding improves productivity [vii]

✓ 87% say buddy programs boost new hire proficiency[viii]

✓ the biggest onboarding challenge is inconsistent application[ix]

✓ the average new hire onboarding experience should consist of 54 activities[x]

Well, we know you're not going to be that kind of leader. So, to help you out, in this chapter, we will give you a framework for building a successful onboarding and training program.

■ DEVELOPING YOUR ONBOARDING PROCESS

The key to a successful start for your new team member is having a meticulously planned onboarding process.

The first two weeks at a company can make or break the experience for a new SDR. Plan in advance. Ensure everything is set up with your human resources or management team so the day your new hire walks into your office or logs in remotely and everything is dialed-in for them and ready to go.

TWO WEEK PLANNING

Mapping out the first two weeks for each new employee is always a positive start. Do it in a spreadsheet or checklist where each hour of the first two is accounted for. This electronic document should link to your playbook[xi] with one click so there is no excuse for you or the new hire to miss anything.

We are challenging you to account for the first two weeks of productivity. It's a far better plan than leaving a new employee alone to struggle, which, unfortunately, is a very common practice. This becomes even more important with everyone working from home.

---

vii　YesElf Onboard News, 7 Statistics That Convince You of Onboarding's Crucial Role, May 20, 2020, *https:// www.yeself.com/sk/onboard-news/82/7-statistics-that-convince-you-of-onboardings-crucial-role*

viii　bambooHR, What New Hires Really Want from Onboarding, p. 5, *https://cdn2.hubspot.net/hubfs/4506945/ Ebook%20URLs/What%20new%20hires%20want%20form%20onboarding%20-%20BambooHR.pdf*

ix　Businesswire, HR's Big Challenge for 2018: Fix New Hire Onboarding, January 16, 2018, *https://www.business-wire.com/news/home/20180116005484/en/HR%E2%80%99s-Big-Challenge-2018-Fix-New-Hire*

x　Jen Dewar, Sapling, 10 Employee Onboarding Statistics You Must Know in 2021, January 4, 2021, *https://www. saplinghr.com/10-employee-onboarding-statistics-you-must-know-in-2021*

xi　Your playbook is a completely documented strategy for running and leading your team. We describe this in detail later in the book.

THE ONBOARDING CHECKLIST

The first part of your onboarding plan should always be the "onboarding checklist." Every company's list will be different, but there are a few things that are standard.

✓ Computer

✓ Desk

✓ Office supplies

✓ Company swag (if you have it)

✓ Logins for all tools

The next part of the checklist varies based on the plan you will outline, so you need to detail the new hire's first two onboarding weeks.

TWO WEEK QUESTIONS

Let's cover what questions should be answered by the end of two weeks. This will allow you to reverse engineer a plan that works for you and your team.

✓ What results are you looking for as a leader, after the first two weeks of on-boarding?

✓ What skills, tools, or techniques should the new employee have at the end of two weeks?

✓ What topics does the SDR need to know and understand to be successful in the role?

✓ What materials should the SDR study during the first two weeks for success?

✓ Who does the SDR need to speak with to learn about the company and its target market?

Once you list out everything needed to answer the questions above, organize them into a document or spreadsheet. This will make it easy for your new hire to stay on track and review all the materials. Each item should be linked to the Onboarding document you created, to make the process simple. You do not want the SDR to have to search for the materials they need.

Having this outline, the SDR will be able to learn about the company and who they serve. Every SDR to be able to quickly learn about the overall industry, its pain points, positions, titles, and other relevant information that determines your prospects.

Training on Personas[xii] and Pain Points is more important than initially concentrating on the intricacies of your product. The faster the SDR learns the attributes of your target customer and the challenges they may face, the faster they will be up and running.

MEETING THE BUSINESS LINE HOLDER

Finally, during the onboarding program, it is important that they meet with the business line holder at your company. This is the person at your company that represents the equivalent of the prospect they will call on.

For example, if their target persona is the Vice President of Sales, your SDR needs to become comfortable engaging the VP in your organization. They should be in regular contact with these people as part of their ongoing training as well.

THE MENTOR PROGRAM

SDRs tend to be social people and enjoy working in groups. In addition, new SDRs thrive when paired up with a more experienced SDR who acts as their mentor. We are strong advocates for having a mentor system.

In addition to assigning each new SDR a high performing SDR as a mentor, assign a high performing AE as well. This AE will guide them through the ups and downs of sales as well as give them guidance on how to make it in sales.

Make sure the SDR meets with each mentor as least once a week for the first month and then once a month after that.

■ BUILDING YOUR SALES DEVELOPMENT PLAYBOOK

The Sales Development Playbook is a critical information repository for running your Sales Development team. It can be either a physical book or an electronic document (both is best). It is the central repository for all knowledge of your company and totally customized to its target client.

---

xii   The term persona is used widely in online and technology applications as well as in advertising as a description of a user of their particular brand.

Here's an outline of what you should include in your Sales Development Playbook.

✓ Company history and overview

✓ Buyer personas and pain points

✓ Business acumen

✓ Product info—how it solves problems for buyers

✓ Approved messaging and templates for practice

✓ Daily life and workflow

✓ Phone and writing skills

✓ Key Performance Indicators

COMPANY HISTORY AND ORGANIZATIONAL INFORMATION

The first part of a good Sales Development Playbook covers the history of the company. This helps each SDR understand the origins of the company and give them context on the founder's "why."

This is also the section that covers your company's mission and vision. Everyone at a company must be aligned with the mission and vision set by the leaders of the company.

Finally, this section should contain organizational information. i.e. who does what at the company. It is not necessary to list every single person. Primarily the heads of each department should be included. This will help the SDR understand how the organization is structured and make getting to the right person for any future questions much easier.

BUYER PERSONAS AND PAIN POINTS

Every SDR on your team must feel strongly that the solutions they offer can help solve their customer's problems. The reason this is so important is that it puts the SDR in a position of strength when they reach out to prospects. The second part of your Playbook should be focused on your buyer, their pain points, and how your solutions help.

Include an outline of your target customer's persona. For example, if you sell a Customer Relationship Management (CRM) solution you may be targeting the VP of Sales, the CEO, and the COOs. For each one of those personas, there should be a description of their role and their relationship with the business challenge or area that you serve. In addition, you should provide more context on each one through relevant questions.

These are questions that you should answer for each persona.

- ✓ What do they like to talk about?
- ✓ What do they think about?
- ✓ What websites do they use often?
- ✓ What software and service tools do they use?
- ✓ What conferences do they attend?
- ✓ What blogs do they read?
- ✓ What webinars do they watch?
- ✓ What problems do they experience?
- ✓ How do they try and solve those problems?
- ✓ What impact does solving these problems have on their business?

All of these items should be listed in the Playbook and be required reading for both new recruits and veteran SDRs. Being knowledgeable and savvy about the industry and the product will ultimately help them be successful.

BUSINESS ACUMEN[XIII]

Another important aspect of training that is often ignored in Sales Development is business acumen. Make sure the playbook familiarizes them with the business problems that the personas are grappling with and the common language that's used.

The easiest way to include this in your Sales Development Playbook is by listing out the common focuses for each persona as well as some common words/phrases that they encounter.

---

xiii   Business acumen is how well someone understands how to deal positively with business situations.

Cyber Security Company

Persona: Network Admin

Pain Points: Bad user behavior, Poor systems integration, System reliability

Persona: CISO

Pain Points: Overall security, Cost containment, Brand image

Persona: Malware Researcher

Pain Points: Understanding current trends, Staying updated, False positives

PRODUCT INFORMATION

At this point, the SDR should have a solid understanding of the personas they will reach out to, their pain points, and the business challenges they are concerned about. To build on this understanding, the next section should cover the high-level overview of how your products or services address those challenges.

Remember, the SDR does not have to understand the intricacies of the product at the same level that an AE must. However, the SDR should know enough about what your products/services do to understand how it solves each of the problems and pain points of the people that they call.

METHODS OF CONVEYING INFORMATION

There are many ways to convey information, such as text, video, podcasts, and quizzes. Your SDR doesn't have to rely only on reading the Playbook. Include as many resources as you think necessary, for each major stipulation.

Make sure it's organized.

*"For Every Minute Spent Organizing,
an Hour Is Earned."*

Benjamin Franklin

APPROVED MESSAGING

In this section of the Playbook, you should provide approved messaging (such as scripts and email templates) for the new SDRs to use.

These will be templates that management has validated as being effective. As the SDR gains experience, they can customize these templates to create their own messaging, including phone scripts for openers, voicemail scripts, scripts for handling objections, email templates, event invitations, and templates for LinkedIn personalized messages.

EXAMPLES OF A GOOD AND A BAD EMAIL:

GOOD:

Hi Name, this is David with Xcorp.

We're talking to (Personas) in the market every day who struggle with (Pain Point), especially during this tough time.

I wanted to see if that was something you are dealing with now, and if I could help. Please shoot back a good time and phone number to reach you.

BAD:

Hi Name,

Our newly released 4RG Technology solution is the highest quality solution for your needs and it's available in your area today. We are ranked the highest in the world in 4RG technology and are number one on the Software Reviews website.

DAILY WORKFLOW

Another section of your Sales Development Playbook should cover daily life and workflow.

Bill Walsh in his book, *The Score Takes Care of Itself*[xiv] (which we highly recommend), stresses the importance of setting high expectations for the team and holding people to those expectations on a daily basis.

"If you set high expectations, but you don't enforce them, you're sending a message that you're not serious about expectations and the success of your team. People follow a leader based on their actions, not sentiments."

---

xiv   Bill Walsh, The Score Takes Care of Itself, Portfolio, June 2010, 10th Edition, np.

Get serious.

Hold your team accountable for the expectations you outlined in the SDR Play-book. Setting expectations but not enforcing them makes you look like an ineffective leader.

THE DAILY CALENDAR

Lay out the daily workflow expectations by including a calendar in the playbook. State what is expected every day, from making phone calls, to sending emails, to doing research, to doing internal meetings, to showing up, and even taking care of personal errands. This is what daily life should look like on the team.

PHONE SKILLS

Having a section of your playbook focused on the basics of being successful on the phone is important. This will allow the SDR to do some self-study to supplement training. As a Sales Development Leader you are responsible for helping your team improve their conversion rates.

A great way to improve the overall conversation rate of your team is to ramp up new hires quickly. Giving a new SDR materials to develop better phone skills, will help them get up to speed quicker. Of course, the faster a new SDR is up and running, the faster they will be able to book meetings (which is good for everyone involved.).

WRITING SKILLS

Writing skills are just as important as phone skills in your SDR Playbook.

Being able to craft well-written messages that sell is a mandatory skill in Sales Development today. Add writing exercises to your playbook to help new SDRs write effectively. This is essential for success in the SDR role, as well as future sales positions and, for that matter, in other aspects of life in general.

For example, have multiple exercises for different parts of an email. We split an email up into four parts. The subject line, hook, body, and call to action (CTA). Have every rep work on each section of an email and let them test it on their prospects. Note: Your reps should be striving for a 50% open rate from their subject line and a 5% response rate from the rest of the email.

KEY PERFORMANCE INDICATORS

Have an outline of what key performance indicators (KPIs) you track. This will ensure that the new SDR will have a clear understanding of the expectations. We even suggest adding an activity calculator so SDRs can calculate how much activity they must do on a daily basis to hit their quota.

INTERNAL SERVICE LEVEL AGREEMENTS[xv]

The playbook should also include an internal Service Level Agreement (SLA), under which the SDR and AE agree on what it means to do certain things and includes definitions of internal vocabulary. These get everyone on the same page as to "who's doing what" and what constitutes success or failure.

For example, a basic SLA should indicate when the meeting with a prospect is acceptable to an AE, and when it will be rejected. The heads of sales, marketing and Sales Development must all agree on these points. SLAs also allows you to adjust the criteria of meetings that you like to see from the Sales Development team based on changes in the marketplace and new ways of thinking about going to market.

SLA DISPUTES

The SDR should feel confident enough to bring the SLA to the AE's attention and ask for clarification if there are disputed points. If there are further issues, they can then bring them up with the manager, who will refer to the SLA to ensure that everyone remains unified on the agreement.

THE TENBOUND SDR PLAYBOOK VALIDATION FRAMEWORK

tenbound.com

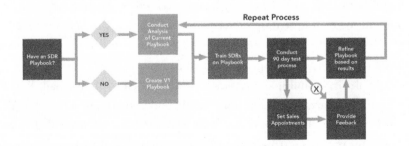

---

xv an internal service level agreement is an SLA that is used to maintain a level of service internally, within an organization, rather than with an external party., Upcouncil, *https://www.upcounsel.com/internal-service-level-agreement*

TAKEAWAYS

✓ Construct and provide a Playbook for all new recruits, that guides them through the basic knowledge they need to be successful on your team.

✓ Create a plan for the entire process in an online spreadsheet that syncs with one click to your SDR Playbook and all onboarding material.

✓ Ensure the weekly meetings are happening between managers and SDRs by setting them on your calendar and providing them with an agenda.

✓ Include role-playing in regular one-on-ones with team members.

✓ Build an effective and consistent training program.

TRAINING AND COACHING

You now have a solid plan in place for onboarding and training new hires. Ongoing training will continue and now we will add a coaching component. What is the difference is between training and coaching?

TRAINING

Training is the process of giving SDRs new skills that they can use to learn and practice in a structured and formatted setting. Training might take place in a conference room as part of a sales kick-off, online and/or delivered by an outside training company.

COACHING

Coaching is the ongoing daily, weekly, and monthly process of ensuring that training is executed and that the SDRs have the guidance they need in order to be successful. It is the ongoing support and refinement of a team that never ends.

Training without coaching is like an email
without a call to action. It's great to have information,
but without knowing how to
use that information, it's useless.

■ BUILDING AN ONGOING TRAINING PROGRAM

The first part of setting up a high-performance ongoing training program for your team is to break out each part of the SDR job into activities.

Ask yourself, *what do SDRs do at each moment of the day, and how can those skills be encouraged, and then perfected, through ongoing training?*

Here is an example of an SDR role breakdown.

- ✓ Prospect research
- ✓ Data input
- ✓ Using tools
- ✓ Writing compelling messages
- ✓ Opening conversations
- ✓ Handling objections
- ✓ Guiding to next steps
- ✓ Interacting with teammates
- ✓ Running reports
- ✓ 1:1 Prep

Create your own breakdown of skills.

Once you have broken out the job function by the activities required, you can then build your training plan around skills improvement for the SDRs in this area.

What gaps in skill development can be amended by using either internal training programs or outside training consultants? Map out a weekly training for each component.

For example, you may notice that the team is excellent in using the tools available in copywriting emails, but they may find it difficult to initiate phone calls and or open conversations. They may be experiencing phone fear.

The initial training program will focus on skill development to ensure they get to the essential skill level. Add to this an ongoing and scheduled coaching program that reinforces the skill learned in training.

According to the book, *Courageous Training: Bold Actions for Business Results* by Tim Mooney and Roger Brinkerhoff[i], knowledge, skills, and attitudes must be instilled through a comprehensive training program and then reinforced through regular coaching and reminders, in order to take hold.

TRACK AND REPORT

When you begin this training program, start with the metrics before training, and then track the metrics post-training. This is how investment in training, especially using outside resources, can be justified to management. This is an important step often overlooked in the rush to achieve a goal.

Since the return on investment of training is difficult to demonstrate, training is usually the first thing to be cut when performance starts to lag. This is strange, in fact counterproductive, because in order to improve the bottom line, performance in some of the skill buckets of the SDR must be improved. However, it is at this point when most companies slash their training budgets. By carefully tracking before and after metrics, you can demonstrate the value of training and coaching and ensure you will get budget approval in the next hiring cycle.

■ DESIGNING YOUR SALES DEVELOPMENT TRAINING PROGRAM

Training is a critical component of a high-performing Sales Development Team. Sometimes, in the rush of our daily lives as managers, training can fall to the wayside.

The key to conducting more training and creating scalable and relevant training materials for your team is first to make a commitment to having a set amount of time per week for team training. One to three hours is what we would recommend at the minimum.

SCHEDULING TRAINING

Training can be part of the team meeting, but no matter when, it has to be scheduled. Plan in advance who will do the training. It doesn't always have to be you. Spread out the responsibility among people within your company— your marketing team, product team, or even outside vendors who do training. Invite thought leaders

---

i   Tim Mooney and Roger O. Brinkerhoff, *Courageous Training: Bold Actions for Business Results*, Berrett-Koehler Publishers, 2008, np.

who will come in and talk to your team about overall industry trends. It's a lot to do it yourself but here is a quick curriculum framework that you can use week after week to ensure you always keep the training relevant.

During your one-on-ones, ask each team member about the top problems they are facing relevant to doing the job. Write down the number one problem across the team.

Finding the main pain point your team is struggling with is how you set the theme for the next training session.

HERE'S A SAMPLE FORMAT:

1. Discuss the problem

2. Give examples of what not to do and errors to avoid

3. More discussion

4. Give a positive example of what to do instead. Teach a new skill

5. Practice role-playing

This type of training structure is most effective because it's always relevant and useful to the people who have been struggling with the challenges they normally face.

It also tells them that you are listening to the issues they are bringing to you and you are directly addressing them through training.

SOLUTIONS YOU FIND BEYOND YOUR OWN KNOWLEDGE

If the problem is something that you don't know how to solve or you haven't been able to find a good solution for it, you now look for someone who can help. It can be someone you bring in from the outside or someone within the company who is particularly skilled in that area.

Leverage your resources.
You don't have to do everything yourself.

THE 5 KEYS TO A ROCK-SOLID SDR TRAINING PROGRAM

You should take the training of your team very seriously. It is a great way to invest in your employees, giving them the skills they need to hit quota, but also to help get them to the next phase in their career. We believe that every SDR has the potential to be great if they are willing to put in the work and hone their craft. We also believe that the better an SDR is, the higher potential they have as an Account Executive. You should train all SDRs with the end goal being a high performing SDR who is primed to be a high-performing Account Executive. There are 5 things we have identified as core to building a strong Sales Development training program.

1: CONSISTENCY

Be consistent in your training plan. When developing a training program, it's important to set a schedule and **STICK TO IT**. This is where we see most SDR teams struggle. The team leader says they are going to do a training session, but the date gets pushed back or totally forgotten. If you value your team and genuinely want them to improve...

Always make time for training.

2: CONTINUAL SUPPORT

In addition to training, SDRs need consistent support to be successful. Every day, SDRs will come across situations that they are unprepared for. When these situations arise, they need someone they can ask for help. If that person isn't always around or never responds, the SDR misses an opportunity to learn and improve.

3: MULTIPLE LEARNING STYLES

A major component of your training program should be the support of multiple learning styles. Everyone learns differently and teaching concepts in multiple ways is a great way to help everyone internalize information. The best way to do this is by switching between traditional role-playing, cold call games, and live call feedback. This way, every SDR gets to interact with the training differently, increasing retention and adoption.

4: REAL WORLD MISSIONS

Our favorite type of training to implement is something we call "real-world missions." Just like how it sounds, this is when the SDR has to physically go out and do something in a public setting or they must use a technique they learned in the real world.

For example, after teaching the SDRs on your team a technique to overcome a "no" or "not interested," from the prospect, instruct them to send you a call recording of them using that technique on a cold call. This clarifies how well the SDR listens and how effectively they use your technique to overcome a negative response.

Another fun one is to have the SDRs go to a local public area with a clipboard and a pen. While there, they must approach strangers and ask them "what is your first impression of me." The reason why this exercise is effective is that oftentimes SDRs get nervous on the phone because they lack confidence and are worried that the prospect is judging them. After doing this exercise they realize that most people have a positive first impression of them and that increases their confidence.

5: PROGRESSION SYSTEM

The last part of the training program that we believe is mandatory to include is having a progression system. Outbound prospecting is difficult to master and If you give advanced prospecting techniques to SDRs who are still learning the basics, they stop doing the basics.

We have seen it time and time again. An SDR begs to know some cool advanced technique and next thing you know, they are messing up simple cold calls in an attempt to try something new.

Don't fall into this trap.

Create a training program that builds on itself and only advances an SDR to the next stage in the progression when you are confident they are ready. We suggest, having exams after completing each major training milestone and for each step you would get a new title and perhaps a raise when they pass, if that is possible at their company. For companies that will not approve a raise, the title is still important as a way to mark progress in their career and not feel stuck. This is very motivational.

A FOUR-STEP REINFORCEMENT
CADENCE FRAMEWORK

STEP 1: THE DAILY STAND-UP

Every day after the team has had a chance to come in and settle or boot up their computer and get a cup of coffee, we suggest you conduct a team stand-up. Have everyone get in a circle or on a video call and talk about how yesterday was, where they are with their numbers, what do they want to accomplish today, and how they plan to get there.

As the leader, you want to take note of how prepared each team member is for this meeting and what their attitude betrays, especially the body language. Are they excited to give detailed plans? Are they crisp and organized? Are they slumped, disheveled, and distracted, without a clear plan for the day?

The people that you identify as being without a clear plan for the day should be taken aside and engaged, i.e. how are they feeling; what's going on? Is there something that you could do to help? If this kind of behavior and attitude continues you want to be aware of it and continually coach people and ensure that they're happy and willing to do the job. The SDR job is challenging and the daily stand-up gives you the time to see how they are doing.

STEP 2: THE WEEKLY ONE-ON-ONE

Every week you should set aside time to have a one-on-one with each one of your reps. Make this a 15 to 20 minute meeting between the SDR and you. The SDR owns the meeting's agenda and must come prepared with their weekly activity and results numbers. They need to understand what they're doing well and where they need some improvement. They should bring with them a game plan for the week to prove they're on track.

PERFORMANCE AND PREPAREDNESS

Another data point in understanding their performance and one where you might see red flags in their attitude is if they come unprepared for the meeting. Holding each SDR on your team to a high standard is imperative and, in your meeting, make sure that they're not merely going through the motions.

PROBLEM RESOLUTION

SDRs will look to you to solve their problems and which, to some extent, you can. However, you have to make it crystal clear that the SDR job is entrepreneurial, and they will need to figure out how to be successful using the tools, resources, and advice that you've given them.

If you're noticing negative behaviors and attitudes of the SDRs in your training sessions, make notes of those behaviors for follow-up.

STEP 3: THE WEEKLY TEAM TRAINING MEETING

While you, as the team leader runs this, the individual SDR's must be in the driver's seat. Every SDR should come prepared as a team and work the agenda that you've laid out for them. Each SDR is expected to deliver a weekly report, including how the week went, addressing any help they need and offering ideas they can share with the group. They also should review the overall numbers. You will discuss training for the week, the month, the quarter, and where it looks like the team is going to end up in relation to the goal.

The meeting is a great time to bring up future motivational contests or events and also company announcements that affect the SDR as employee. The beginning part of the meeting should last about 30 minutes; the remaining 30 minutes can be training led by the manager or one of the SDR's. This training should address one of the skill gaps that you're seeing with your team.

Training topics can include:

- ✓ Opening a call
- ✓ Handling objections
- ✓ Closing for the appointment
- ✓ How to motivate yourself to make more calls
- ✓ Research accounts
- ✓ Any identifiable skill gaps

Remember, you can give each team member a topic and have them run a training session in a skill area where they excel.

TEAM IDENTIFICATION

Your meeting will tell you:

- ✓ Who are the leaders?
- ✓ Who are the followers?
- ✓ Who are the people who are actively bringing down the energy of the team and consistently being negative?

This is a way for you to keep your pulse on the team and accelerate the process of improvement.

STEP 4: AD HOC TRAINING

Next up in the coaching cadence is ad hoc training, or training to meet the specific needs identified by the team meeting. This is a lot of fun and relieves some of the pressure on you to come up with a new training plan each week.

CREATIVE AD HOC

Be creative. Bring in an outside trainer who specializes in one of the skills you've identified. Don't be confined by the usual sales training options that are out there. Think about training your team in copywriting and video presentations. Consider improv exercises, role-playing, and many of the different ways that they could practice interacting with people.

Training is a great opportunity to bring in industry thought leaders, not only people in the area of Sales Development, but other experts who are relevant to your field and the product.

FOR EXAMPLE

Invite industry experts to address your team. Have technical people from your company do a demonstration or chat about what they're working on. What does a day in their life look like and what exciting things are they working on? What are their pain points? Where do they see the industry going?

Bring in the person in your company who is parallel to the actual buyer persona. For example, if your SDRs are calling on CFOs, invite your own CFO to talk about what their daily life looks like and what their challenges are. How do they interact with sales development representatives and what kind of information are they looking for?

Your team will get a good idea about what it's like in the world they are targeting and the experience will add value to their conversations.

USING OUTSIDE SALES TRAINERS

The field of sales has many outside training options, each with its specific expertise. Paid training consultants can help give another perspective to your team. By reinforcing their training, you can see great results.

If you choose to go this route, be sure to meet with the sales trainer and explain how your team is set up and your specific needs. Make sure they are not just following a template that they use at every company and, very important, you should preview the curriculum before committing to the training.

A fully customized program is costly and probably not necessary in most cases. For instance, if they have a template that is effective for cold calling and it works for many other companies, then it might not need to be customized for your company. The trainer coming in should understand, at a high level, how their template framework would translate to your business objectives.

Spend time with the trainer to determine whether their training would be a good fit culturally. You certainly don't want to put the wrong personality in front of your team.

■ BUILDING YOUR COACHING PROCESS

Think about the greatest sports teams on earth. Would you expect their coaches to simply train the team for a week or two at the beginning of the season and then tell them to go out and play without any further coaching? Never. A truly successful team has a program of continuous training and coaching—scheduled, quantified, and data-driven.

GOOD COACHING

One of the best ways to get good at coaching is to study great coaches and understand what they do to support their teams.

Bill Walsh, Bill Belichick, John Wooden, and Vince Lombardi are just some of the more successful sports coaches known around the world. You may remember teachers or coaches from your childhood and at school who made a big difference to you. The best coaches are tough and demand high standards, but also parallel that with warmth and love for their team members.

As the team coach, you must strive to strike a balance between high expectations and warmth and empathy.

COACHING CADENCE

To manage a high-performance Sales Development team, it is vital that your calendar reflect a regularly set coaching cadence. What that means is that it must have a regular and repeated patter. Furthermore, you must hold yourself accountable for that cadence. This is the key job and leverage point for a Sales Development Leader.

COACHING PROCESS SETUP

There are two fundamental approaches to the coaching process setup.

1. You run the process yourself. This is the most hands-on method. You have first-hand knowledge of the efficiency of the processes you put in place. You will know where the bottlenecks are and what needs to be addressed.

Doing this will build credibility with your team. You have established that you are not a hands-off dilettante residing in an ivory tower— you are an actual practitioner who knows the job better than anyone else. You walk the walk and talk the talk. You show everyone on the team that you can actually execute on the recommendations you're giving them.

When your team sees you as credible, it's easier to improve processes that you're putting in place. When you show the team that you can do the job and that you care about improving the process, you have scored a double win.

2. Your coaching schedule must include regular inspections of the team's work. These inspections should happen all the time—when they make phone calls, when they talk with gatekeepers and prospects, when they send emails, or replying to emails. You will ascertain their social media reach, and their attendance at live events where they talk to real prospects.

In your coaching practice, these touchpoints should be addressed on a regular basis.

LET'S DISCUSS HOW THIS WOULD LOOK FOR COACHING PHONE CALLS, EMAILS, AND CALENDARS.

PHONE CALLS

It is important to ensure that your team has mastery over the first five to ten seconds of a phone call. Sales Development teams can sometimes call 100 or 200 people without actually making contact. So, when one of those precious conversations does happen, the SDR must nail it in the first five to 10 seconds.

Think of it as a chain. You must have the first link in order to create the chain or no results will ensue. This is so important. You don't need an advanced technology solution to monitor that first five to ten seconds. Sit with the SDR and connect in to the phone they're having. Remember, this is time-consuming because it may take one to 200 dials before reaching one prospect, so plan your listening time in advance.

CALL RECORDING SOFTWARE

In order to maximize your time, you can use call recording software to record the call and analyze it later. Several firms offer products like this and they can save you a tremendous amount of time that would otherwise be spent waiting for someone to answer the phone. You're looking for is a scorecard of how the initial five to 10 seconds transpire on the phone. Have your SDRs bring in their call recordings to your one-on-ones and review what went well and what could be improved.

PRACTICE

In addition to monitoring, it's always a good idea to practice phone calls with your SDRs through role-playing. At any time in your one-on-one team meeting or another appropriate time, you simply ask the SDR to sit down and then, you say, "I am persona X at company X. You just called me and I just picked up the phone to answer. Go." In other words, you give them the signal to start their five-second spiel.

Keep track of how they do during these sessions. Are they improving? Are they still flustered? As a coach, your main goal is to guide them past being flustered until they speak easily.

Later in this chapter, we will outline how you can run role-plays.

LEAD BY EXAMPLE

We have another suggestion, and most SDR leaders won't do it. As the SDR Leader, it is important that you make calls yourself every day. No matter how busy you are, carve out at least one hour in the morning in the same area that your Sales Development Reps are working.

They must hear you on the phone making the calls. Make mistakes; screw up; let them know that they don't have to be perfect but that they need to continue to make calls.

A friendly competition between SDRs and the Team Leader to see who books the most meetings is a great way to boost confidence and show that you're willing to do what you ask them to do.

COLD EMAIL

Abundant research about effective cold emails demonstrates that it's easy to tie data to the success of the email. Through many systems, you can check how well emails are performing. The key to email success is to have control over the number being sent over a certain time period. This will quantify the conversion rates that you are looking for.

THE LAYERED APPROACH

Although it's tempting, our recommendation is not to let the SDRs run their own email campaigns without some control from the team leader. Control depends on the seniority of the SDR. New SDRs should have less control over the content of their emails. The most successful teams have this layered approach—more oversight for new SDRs and less for seasoned ones.

OVERSIGHT FOR SEASONED AND NEWER SDRS

For an SDR with little experience, emails are created by executives or content marketers in a specific way to support a specific message. As that SDR gains more experience and success, they're given more leeway to create their own messaging. Eventually, as an acknowledgment of their progress, they are allowed to add more of their own personality to their email campaigns.

HOW DO YOU COACH EMAIL EFFECTIVENESS?

As a team leader, you may be asking yourself this question and this is how you need to approach it.

First, ask the SDRs to bring, what we call, their latest email volley[ii]. Read the email that was sent. Review the template the SDR used for email content. Ensure that the communication is up to the standards that you would subscribe to for your team's performance.

There's nothing worse than having an angry executive come up to you and say, "What on earth are your SDRs doing? Look at this terrible email they're sending. Are you even running this team?

THE CALENDAR

Another important aspect of each team is the calendar. Many SDRs may not know the important aspect here is that the calendar is sacred. You must ensure that SDRs block out their most important and proactive activities on their calendar.

CALENDAR REQUIREMENTS

Ensure that each SDR's calendar is set up to reflect the most difficult tasks they must complete every day. For instance, making cold calls, sending customized emails, and doing account research.

WILLPOWER AND CALENDAR ENTRIES

Your willpower is like a battery on your phone—you have only a certain amount of juice throughout the day and that juice becomes gradually depleted as time passes. It is important to teach the SDR's the need to schedule the first part of the day with the most difficult task that need to be accomplished.

That calendar time is absolutely sacred and during that time, permit no meetings, no social events, no nothing except for the hard work your SDRs must do during those time slots. Once those time periods are over more unstructured activities can be scheduled to take place.

Early time periods are important. They should be dedicated to calling tasks. Insist that calling times be prioritized and, most important that the SDR actually follow what the calendar says.

We've all put a new exercise routine or other positive activity on the calendar, just to have it pop up every day and then, get ignored.

Completion of our daily rituals move us forward toward higher goals.

---

ii   A volley is an email the SDR sent that received a response from the prospect. The prospect then responded to this, the SDR responded to their response, and the prospect then answered back. Think of the interplay as volleying in volleyball.

"You are what you do, not what you say you'll do."

— Carl Gustav Jung

ROLE-PLAYING AND HOW IT WORKS

Adding role-playing to coaching is the key to ensuring the high performance of your team. Is is time-consuming and sometimes painful for most sales development leaders, so, unfortunately, it gets skipped.

Role-playing exercises are uncomfortable, awkward, and time-consuming for everyone, but just as blocking and tackling are the building blocks of a good football team, role-playing is the foundation of an ongoing coaching program for SDRs.

HOW DO I SET UP A GOOD ROLE-PLAY PROGRAM?

SCHEDULE ROLE-PLAY TIMES

The first step is always to make time for it. Role-playing with your entire team should become a regular calendar entry. Once you have the time committed, follow through.

Good role-playing exercises start with proper preparation.

ROLE-PLAY PREP

FOR YOU

When preparing for the role-play it's important to map out the three target personas, their characteristics, and their main pain points as related to your product or service. You will need to understand what makes the target persona tick, what keeps him/her up at night, and how your phone call, email, or social touch will fit into their daily work life. Put all this information into a document you can easily reference during a role play.

FOR YOUR SDRS

They should know the context of their communication. Why are they calling? Why is it important to each specific persona? How will it improve the prospect's work life? Make sure you are on the same page with the rep on all these points.

BASICS OF ROLE-PLAYING

During a role-play session, it is very important for you not to break character. You must embody the persona the SDR is "calling" and you must respond realistically to the SDR. This will be uncomfortable and they will not like it. Maybe you won't either but it's a labor of love. You want the SDR to be successful and making the role-play as lifelike and realistic as you possibly can is how you make the most out of the exercise.

DON'T BE NICE ABOUT IT

A role-play is not the time to be nice. In the real world, prospects are busy and not expecting your call. They will be curt or even rude to the SDR when the connection is made. The point of role-playing is to make the conversation as difficult as possible for the SDR, so it helps them build the muscle they need to survive the call. Otherwise, it's a waste of time.

CHALLENGE THE SDR

During the exercise, you want to test the SDR's ability to handle adversity without getting defensive or upset. Create so much discomfort that when they are in a real situation, they don't choke and they can stay focused.

We want them to be used to operating in a highly tense environment on the phone so that they can get enough oxygen in the conversation to be able to continue their message without getting overly rattled.

GIVING FEEDBACK

The feedback section is really the third phase of the role-playing exercise. Gather up your notes and give the rep a lot of praise for what they did well. After the positive feedback, give them two things they could improve on, three at the most. Make a note for yourself and follow up in your next scheduled one-on-one meeting. This is a great way to see if they're actually using the tips and techniques that you've given them or if it's going in one ear and out the other.

■ PERFORMANCE MANAGEMENT

With all the training and coaching you are now doing, performance issues will inevitably come up. When it comes to performance management, follow a structured format religiously. This structured format should include a one-on-one schedule, as well as the team meetings and other interactions that you've established with the SDR.

There are three main factors in your performance management process:

1. Attitude
2. Metrics
3. Team Impact

ATTITUDE

Attitude is absolutely the most important element of performance. You could have someone with excellent metrics but has a negative, rebellious, or dismissive attitude. This individual is a challenge to lead and their negativity will be draining to you as their leader.

METRICS

When setting up your performance management structure it's critical to have a spreadsheet where you can review details of each one-on-one and various performance issues. This spreadsheet records how they're doing from a metrics and teamwork perspective.

TEAM IMPACT

Make sure to note how the SDR is impacting the team. Are they a net positive or a drag on morale? Document everything that you can on an ongoing basis for both positive and negative performance reasons.

TAKE NOTES

You always want to have notes on what people are doing right so that you can share that with the team and the rest of the company, when appropriate. This will promote the fact that you're leading well and your people are happy.

If an individual's performance starts to slip to the point that they must be "written up" on what's called a performance improvement plan (PIP), it is imperative that you document all of your conversations with that person from a legal perspective. Take meticulous notes throughout the process and record them via Google Docs, Evernote, or just a Word document.

SETTING UP A PERFORMANCE IMPROVEMENT PLAN

People get into Sales Development for a lot of reasons. For some, it's the hunt and the thrill of connecting with new prospects. Others love talking about the value of your products and services.

Not everyone enjoys an SDR role, once they're in it. For those individuals, the job itself becomes a trap in a nightmare that becomes their daily lives. This is obviously not a great thing for anybody involved and certainly, not you as the team leader. The purpose of the Sales Development team is to generate new sales opportunities for the business. Every SDR must be able to achieve that.

As the leader, you might find yourself in a situation when the metrics, attitude, and/or teamwork are not meeting your standards. The sports coach analogy comes into play once again. You must strive to have the best team on the field and that requires you to run a high-performance program.

THE IMPORTANCE OF DOCUMENTATION

First and foremost, when consider putting an underperforming SDR on a performance improvement plan, it's essential you have all of your documentation recorded. Expect your HR department to ask you for it. You should have all of your notes, showing metrics, attitude, and/or teamwork should be ready to substantiate the lack of performance.

STAKEHOLDER INVOLVEMENT

Be sure to involve all the stakeholders as early as possible. This includes your boss, other concerned executives, and anyone who might be involved in the individual's employment.

SDR COMMUNICATION

Communicate the performance improvement plan with the SDR. Keep the conversation open and honest.

TRANSPARENCY

Being open and transparent with the SDR is critical. You never want performance issues to be a surprise to anyone. There's nothing worse than sitting in a meeting with someone who's expecting thanks for doing a great job and has idea that you're actually disappointed with their results. This experience typically happens with a leader who is friends with everyone and subsequently is just too nice to let them know when they are not performing up to standard.

OPEN COMMUNICATION AND HONESTY

These are the most important traits of a Sales Development Leader. The job is to communicate openly and honestly with people both up and down the chain of command. They should never let sub-standard performance be a surprise.

Don't forget...

A performance improvement plan is not the end of a person's employment or a death sentence for the person at the company. We have seen it multiple times—an SDR is put on a performance review plan and then proceeds to perform according to the requirements stated in the plan. Happily, that SDR stays on track with a great attitude and eventually comes off the performance improvement plan and remains employed by the company.

A performance review plan can be a wake-up call for an SDR who perhaps wasn't taking the job seriously or had lost interest in the product for a while. That individual just needed a nudge to get back on track. That's the purpose of a performance review plan. They encourage these individuals to get back on track as quickly as possible.

Remember...

NEVER judge an SDR because they've had performance issues. As the leader, this is your responsibility as much as it is theirs.

You may find yourself in a situation where an overbearing VP or another executive may insist you fire or reprimand someone on your team. Remember, you need the freedom and authority to run the program in the most effective way for you and your company. It's your program, you are the leader.

Healthy conflict is good for an organization. If your superior is giving you bad advice or advice not backed up by anything but his or her opinion, it's ok to push back. Bring your data and demonstrate it in a respectful way. If they continue to insist, you may have to bend to their wishes in order to stay employed, or realize the situation you're in is not a great fit for you and move on elsewhere.

The point is...

It's your ship.

■ A FRAMEWORK FOR DEVELOPING TOP-PERFORMING SDRS

VOURIS 3 MONTH SDR TRAINING FRAMEWORK OUTLINE

Dates	Session	Topics		
7/20/XX	**Prospecting Strategy**	Sequences	Prospect needs analysis	Organizing your day
7/23/XX	**Account and Prospect Grading**	Adjusting account grade	Improving lead discovery	Prospect priority framework
7/27/XX	**Cold Call Strategy**	Structure of a cold call	Why cold calling works	How to handle rejection
7/30/XX	**Cold Call Role Play**	Role play cold calls		
8/3/XX	**Overcoming Brush-Offs**	The Triple A	Timing	Brush-off vs. objection
8/6/XX	**Overcoming Brush-Offs Role Play**	Practice overcoming brush-offs		
8/10/XX	**Cold Email Basics**	Structure of a cold email	Subject lines	Follow up
8/13/XX	**Cold Email Workshop**	Review emails with feedback		
8/17/XX	**Mindset**	what to do when it gets tough	Avoid negativity	Celebrate all wins
8/20/XX	**Cold Call Role Play**	Practice cold calls		
8/24/XX	**Getting through the gatekeeper**	Different types of gatekeepers	Best script I've found	Being dynamic
8/27/XX	**Role Play Gatekeepers**	Role play getting through gatekeepers		
8/31/XX	**Managing Accounts**	How to organize accounts	Taking advantage of their org structure	Prioritization
9/3/XX	**Cold Call Role Play**	Role play cold calls		
9/7/XX	**LinkedIn Prospecting**	Connection requests	Messaging types	Sales navigator
9/10/XX	**Sequencing Workshop**	Review sequences with feedback		
9/14/XX	**Priority Notetaking**	How to track cold calls effectively	Prioritize what to say next	Logging information
9/17/XX	**Role Play Cold Call With Priority Notetaking**	Practice using priority note taking on a cold call		
9/21/XX	**Optimizing workflow with data**	What KPIs are you tracking?	What is your biggest area to improve	Using data to enhance your strategy
9/24/XX	**Cold Email Workshop**	Review emails with feedback		
9/28/XX	**Researching Prospects**	3x3 research framework	Tailoring emails with research	When NOT to research
10/1/XX	**Improving vocal tonality**	Create your cold call character	Vocal variety	Using tone to show authority
10/5/XX	**Role play tonality**	Practice using tone		
10/8/XX	**Prospecting 101 Exam**	Exam to graduate from Prospecting 101 to Advance Prospecting (Vouris Training Progression)		

TAKEAWAYS

✓ Establish a coaching cadence and stick to it.

✓ Consistently conduct role-playing exercises.

✓ Institute a performance improvement program.

✓ Establish and schedule an ongoing training program.

ANALYSIS

Sales Development is a combination of art and science. The art is the classic Sales "soft skills[i]" you'll need to teach your team to ensure their success.

The science part is how you organize your team to get the business results your company requires. This includes the tracking and experimentation that is required to consistently achieve those results.

■ CALCULATING SDR TEAM EXPECTATIONS

If your company doesn't have clear activity expectations outlined for the SDR team, you must go through the process of determining what those expectations should be. To begin this process, break down your goals based on the end results you're looking for from the team. Reverse engineer from goal setting, all the way to the daily activities.

We have a simple, four-step process for doing this.

STEP 1: DETERMINE WHAT PERCENTAGE OF REVENUE YOUR TEAM IS RESPONSIBLE FOR

This is simple. You must understand the revenue that the Sales Development team is responsible for. This number will be how you will create the goals for your team and give you the clarity required to make sure the expectations are aligned with the desired result: revenue.

In order to determine goals for revenue production, you will need to work with senior leadership to clarify the total revenue expectation for the sales team and what percentage of the team's revenue is expected to come from SDR-generated opportunities.

---

i These are informal abilities that are learned over a person's lifetime and usually relate to the person's aptitude in performing common tasks and connecting with other people. *www.saleshacker.com/sales-skills-traits/*

If your company expects every deal to come from your team, 100%, the total sales revenue number, is what you are ultimately responsible for. If the company expects 50% of the deals to have been generated by the SDR Team, cut that revenue number in half.

Don't let it become a roadblock if you can't get an exact number. The program must have a goal in order to build an action plan to achieve it. As the leader you must be able to help create that goal. Use any data you have available and come up with the goal yourself.

STEP 2: IDENTIFY HOW MUCH PIPELINE IS NEEDED TO HIT THE REVENUE GOAL

Once you have the revenue percent your team is responsible for, it's time to calculate how much pipeline it takes to achieve that number. There are a few ways to calculate this, but let's use the simplest method for this exercise.

Take the amount of revenue that the entire sales team is responsible for, divide by the average deal size to get how many deals are needed to achieve the revenue goal.

[REVENUE] / [AVERAGE DEAL SIZE] = DEALS NEEDED TO HIT REVENUE TARGET

STEP 3: CALCULATE THE CLOSE RATE

You've estimated the number of deals needed to hit the revenue goal, so now, calculate how many sales opportunities your team will need for the sales team to meet that revenue goal.

To do this, calculate the close percentage for deals, from the stage where the hand-off from the SDR to AE takes place. Let's use "demonstration" for this example.

A "quick and dirty" way of calculating this is to take how many closed deals there were last year and divide that by how many demos took place.

[CLOSED DEALS] / [HOW MANY DEMOS TOOK PLACE] = CLOSE %

This will give you an estimate of the close rate on demonstrations. Senior leadership should have this number for you, but if they don't know and you do not have historical data, use an estimate based on industry standards.

STEP 4: CALCULATE WHAT THE SDR TEAM MUST PRODUCE IN ONE YEAR

We should now have all the numbers we need to calculate what the SDR team is responsible for. All that's left is to actually do that math.

Here's a simple equation:

**([DEALS NEEDED TO HIT REVENUE TARGET]
X [EXPECTATION OF % DEALS GENERATED FROM SDRS])
/ [CLOSE %]
= NUMBER OPPORTUNITIES THE SDR TEAM IS RESPONSIBLE FOR**

Take all the numbers you've gathered from each step and plug them into the above equation. What number did you come up with?

Let's do an example together.

SDR GENERATED PIPELINE EXPECTATION

50%
Sales Revenue Goal
$5,000,000
Average Deal Size
$30,000
Close Percent
20%

Deals needed to hit revenue target
$5,000,000 / $30,000 =
167

SDR Team Goal
(167 X 50%) / 20% =
418
discovery/demos/etc.

Take your calculation and spread it across the number of months and the number of SDRs you have.

So, we divide 418 by 12 to get 35 and divide that by 4 to get 9. That means, for our example above, that they would need each SDR to get 9 meetings a month to hit their revenue target.

If you do this math and the final number you get isn't possible, you need to have a tough conversation about greater resource allocation toward your program. This may include more tools, better training, hiring more SDRs, potentially outsourced assistance, and/or research assistants to accelerate the program.

There's nothing more unmotivating for a Sales Development team than being handed a number that is commonly known to be impossible to hit.

WARNING

We've seen many Sales Development Leaders get fired for not getting ahead of this conversation early in the process.

As the leader, you must be able to demonstrate the math used to calculate the number to everyone involved in achieving it, including executives, partners, and your team. If the number is too high, it's up to you to ensure that everyone understands you're going to either need greater resource allocation, or more realistic goals. Remember, your job might be at stake as well as your success in executing the plan.

EXECUTION

We have our pipeline goal and we understand the timeline.

It's time to execute.

To hit that pipeline goal, you can break it down in this way:

- ✓ How many appointments will you need?
- ✓ In which categories?
- ✓ In which verticals?
- ✓ What time frame is optimal?
- ✓ Do you have the resources to be able set these appointments?

And even more vital questions:

- ✓ What support will you have from marketing?
- ✓ What is the forecast for lead flow?
- ✓ What assistance do you have to select accounts in a strategic way? (Account-Based Sales Development)

✓ Are there key pieces of information that are missing in your database that you need in order to set these appointments?

✓ Are there any events coming up or support that you can ask for from your field marketers in order to achieve this number?

✓ Can you use outsourced SDR programs to augment the work of your team?

SIDE NOTE ONE: Don't be afraid of outsourced SDR programs. They can be invaluable to you in augmenting missing information and activities. They can help you make your number. Marketing and project managers, as well as others, use outsourced programs all the time.

SIDE NOTE TWO: Industry benchmarks can be a handy starting point and interesting comparison, but each company's market and vertical[ii] is different. So, use them as guideposts only and then, quickly create your own TAM funnel and identify your own bottlenecks. Once those are defined you can begin to tackle them.

■ USING OUTSOURCED SDR SERVICES

We have never seen an outsourced firm hired that has completely replaced the in-house Sales Development team. Certainly, we have seen executives get tired of low performing, in-house teams and then, scrap the program, only to rebuild it after completely outsourced lead generation doesn't meet their expectations.

When companies move forward with outsourced lead generation, they find that the outsourced company not only cannot set the right number and volume of appointments, they also lose the benefit of bringing in top talent to the company to create the leaders of tomorrow. This is why we never see outsourced lead generation totally replace an internal team. However, we do see the two work in conjunction with one another.

---

ii   A vertical market is a market in which vendors offer goods and services specific to an industry, trade, profession, or other group of customers with specialized needs. *https://en.wikipedia.org/wiki/Vertical_market.*

WHEN TO CONSIDER OUTSOURCED
SDR SERVICES

When it comes to using outsourced SDR Services, make sure that you have an efficient method to get the information gathered by the outsourced program into your database. There is a tremendous amount of energy expended gathering information, but it's wasted when that data does not make it into the CRM or any organized database.

You need to have access to the information gathered by the outsourced company as it could be vital in determining your target market, ideal customer profile, and best messaging.

■ WHAT METRICS SHOULD YOU BE TRACKING?

Before we talk about what SDR metrics to track, let's define what they are and why we should be monitoring them in the first place.

SALES ACTIVITY METRICS:

This allows you to monitor the activities of your SDR team and better understand what impact they will have on the future.

> *When it comes to sales, today's activities are*
> *tomorrow's performance.*

TRANSPARENCY AND ACCOUNTABILITY

There are two things you must do on a daily basis.

✓ Identify what is working today so you can repeat it tomorrow.

✓ Identify what is underperforming today so that you can improve it before tomorrow.

Although the above is what you should be doing daily, holding your team accountable to metrics also has an impact on them.

When your SDR team knows what sales activities are being tracked, they will aim to increase their performance. The reason is not that they are being watched by "big brother." It's because there is transparency in what they must do, as an individual, to hit their number and maximize their compensation. Transparency and accountability allow you, as the leader, to prioritize your coaching.

For example, if you see that someone is doing all the right activity, but they aren't hitting their targets, you can use the data to identify where they need help. This wouldn't be possible if they were hitting their activity levels because you would not have enough data to be confident in what's holding them back. Are they struggling with sales conversations or are they simply not doing enough activity?

Overall, the sales metrics you hold your SDR team accountable to gives you much more insight into how you can improve and optimize your prospecting strategy for higher success rates.

WHERE TO LOOK FOR CHANGE

✓ Look at your existing SDR team data and see if you can answer this question: "What do I need to change to guarantee that we hit our quota?"

✓ Where are the bottlenecks I can remove in order to increase performance?

We group tracking sales metrics into two main categories.

1. Input Metrics
2. Output Metrics

INPUT METRICS

Inputs are a quantity metric that allows you to track the number of results. It answers questions like, "how many meetings will we book this month" and "What percentage of conversations lead to a scheduled meeting?"

OUTPUT METRICS

Output is a quality metric that allows you to track the quality of your team's meetings. It answers questions such as, "how many meetings does it take to close a deal" and "how much revenue does each SDR generate a year?"

SIX KEY SALES DEVELOPMENT METRICS YOU SHOULD TRACK

There are six key metrics that we recommend you track and monitor regularly. There are a lot of metrics you can be tracking but using the ones I cover here will allow you to quickly evaluate the health of your team and allow you to understand the quality of meetings your team is setting. It will help keep your team on track by having minimum activity expectations. In our opinion, having a standardized activity expectation is mandatory. Many SDR Managers don't hold their team accountable to minimum expectations, so the metric and the manager, become pointless.

THE SIX METRICS

1. Calls Made & Call Outcome
2. Emails Sent & Email Outcome
3. Meetings Scheduled
4. Future Meetings
5. Sales Accepted Opportunities (SAO)
6. Revenue

CALLS MADE & OUTCOME

Tracking the number of calls and their outcomes is a great way to keep your finger on the pulse of what's happening with each individual on your team.

There are two primary reasons why this metric is helpful.

1. You can quickly identify who needs cold call coaching.
2. You can quickly identify if there are problems with your call list.

To track this metric, you need to know how many calls are being made and what the outcomes of those calls are. The outcomes include (no answer, connected, initial meeting scheduled, disqualified, etc.)

TRY THIS: Look at the connect to meeting scheduled rate for each SDR on your team. Find the average and coach those who are falling behind.

EMAILS SENT & OUTCOME

In the same way you are tracking calls, you should also be tracking emails and their outcomes.

There are two primary reasons why this metric is helpful.

1. You can quickly identify who needs coaching on email.
2. You can quickly identify if there are problems with your email list.

To track this metric, you need to know how many emails are being sent and what the outcomes of those emails are. The outcomes include (no reply, replied, initial meeting scheduled, disqualified, etc.).

Look at the email sent to meeting scheduled rate for each SDR on your team. Find the average and coach those who are falling behind.

MEETINGS SCHEDULED

This metric is one of the most important because is is an indicator that your team is or is not on track. In addition, it allows you to identify if other inputs are leading to enough meetings to meet expectations.

EXAMPLE:

If the activity to meeting scheduled rate is low, you should do some training or provide a new leads list.

By contrast, this metric can also be used to discover new messaging or processes that are leading to better results.

EXAMPLE:

If an SDR is performing extremely well, you can analyze what they are doing and share it with the rest of the team to improve their results.

Look at the activity to meeting set rate for each member of your team and analyze what the top performers are doing that sets them apart from the rest.

FUTURE MEETINGS

The future meetings metric will allow you to forecast how your team will do against quota. If this metric is low, you will have to motivate your team to increase inputs. If this metric is high, things are looking good and you should use that to keep your team motivated.

This is what you should do. Look at how many future meetings your team has and, based on historical math, where will you end up against quota?

SALES ACCEPTED OPPORTUNITY (SAO)[III]

Tracking this metric will allow you to determine how good the quality of leads that your SDRs are generating.

If the percentage of meetings your team books to the number of SAOs is high, the quality is high. If this rate is low, the quality is low. Keep in mind, the goal isn't a 100% meeting to SAO rate. This rate will vary from company to company but should be based on the Account Executives workload. The more time the AEs have, the more you should prioritize quantity. They less time they have, the more you should prioritize quality.

Look at the meeting to SAO (situation action outcome) rate for each individual on your team. Does anyone stand out? If so, what are they doing differently?

REVENUE

This is every sales leader's favorite word… **REVENUE.**

Tracking the revenue that each SDR is responsible for does two things.

1. Shows the impact that the team has on the company.

2. Justifies further investment in the SDR team.

This is the ultimate quality metric and should be treated as such. This metric can be used to motivate your team, convince leadership to invest more, and prove your value as a leader.

HOW DO YOU TRACK THESE SALES METRICS?

Tracking the input and output metrics of your Sales Development team is as simple as setting up some reports in the CRM. Each CRM is different so instead of a technical walkthrough, let's cover how to track each one of these metrics.

CALLS MADE & OUTCOME

The phone system you use should be logging calls directly into the CRM. Make sure every call is logged and that each SDR is required to select a "call outcome" from

---

iii   A qualified sales lead.

a drop-down menu. Create a report of all calls made within a specific timeframe and organize it by the outcome.

EMAILS SENT & OUTCOME

Your email service provider should be integrated with your CRM and logging all emails. Make sure every email is logged and that you are tracking opens, clicks, and replies.

Create a report of all emails sent within a specific timeframe and organize it by opens, clicks, and replies. Finally, run a separate report of Meetings Scheduled where the last activity was an email. This will show you how many meetings are getting scheduled from the emails your team is sending.

MEETINGS SCHEDULED

Every SDR must be responsible for logging meetings when they schedule them. Make sure you are having the SDRs update those meetings with their outcome (no-show, SAO, Disqualified, etc.).

Create a report that shows how many meetings were scheduled within a specific timeframe and organizes it by rep and by how it was scheduled (phone, email, LinkedIn, etc.).

FUTURE MEETINGS

The future meetings report is a simple report that will help you better forecast what the month or quarter will look like. Again, this requires every SDR to be logging their meetings in the CRM.

Create a report of all meetings with a future meeting date within the month or quarter you are focused on and organize it by SDR who scheduled it.

SALES ACCEPTED OPPORTUNITY

The core metric that SDR teams are held accountable for. To track this metric the AE must mark meetings that they conduct as "sales accepted."

Create a report of all sales accepted opportunities that were a result of an SDR scheduled meeting and organize this report by SDR.

REVENUE

Tracking the revenue generated by each member of your team requires is simple and every CRM I know of makes it easy to do.

Create a report of all the closed deals that were started by an SDR scheduled meeting and organize this report by SDR.

■ UNDERSTANDING THE TENBOUND SALES DEVELOPMENT TAM (Total Addressable Market) FUNNEL

Now that you've learned how to calculate your goals and monitor your performance, let's break down what goes into creating those appointments at your company.

Understanding how to customize your Sales Development program to fit the company that you work for is critical.

The easiest way to think about Sales Development metrics is to set up The Tenbound Sales Development TAM Funnel in relation to the different verticals and account sizes that your Sales Development team targets.

As you can see, the funnel illustrates, in a simple graphic, how to look at your marketplace and organize your Sales Development approach strategically, whether you're going inbound or outbound.

The spaces between the funnel stages represent breakpoints in the process. Each is a time-consuming step for the Sales Development team. As the manager, your job is to identify and release these points as they arise.

TAM (TOTAL ADDRESSABLE MARKET) POTENTIAL CUSTOMERS

At the top of the funnel is your total addressable market, the TAM. These are all the customer accounts (organizations, such as companies) out there that might intentionally buy your product or service. The easiest way to do this is to divide this potential addressable market at the top of the funnel into A B C and D.

A: These accounts are your dream accounts that you would love to bring to your business. These are the ones that could make a huge difference in your quarter, your year, or the life of your company. These will be highest on your priority list.

B: These pay the bills. They may not be your ideal accounts and they may not be a game-changer for your business, but they are an important part. They are the meaty part, the high point of the bell curve.

C: You would never go after these proactively. Perhaps they are in the wrong industry or are too small, or too niched. However, if they are interested in using your product and service, and come to you as an inbound lead, they should be engaged.

D: These entities are too small or too complicated or they're in verticals where you have little or no experience. You will never sell to these companies and you should ignore them.

Each of the A, B, C, and D accounts and each vertical that you go after will potentially have its own TAM funnel. For example, if you're going after the high-tech sector, it will have its own TAM funnel, or if you're going after the government sector, it too will have its own TAM funnel.

Every vertical or sector will have its own TAM. Do not try to use the same funnel for your whole market or things can get confusing, and your efforts will not be as effective.

ORGANIZATION OF ACCOUNTS

Now, the critical, hard work begins. Working with your executive team and your marketing team, you must organize the accounts to align with ABCD in order to maximize the time of your Sales Development team.

We see too many teams skip this part and the Sales Development team spends its time on the wrong accounts. We've seen teams working on accounts that should be in the D range. This is wasting time by talking to people who will never buy your product. This is especially the case with inbound leads, because they need to be triaged in the same way. When an inbound lead comes in, SDRs should identify and mark its account level as A, B, C, or D.

The Sales Development team on the outbound side should spend time working selectively on A and B accounts. If you have a hybrid or inbound team, they can work on C accounts that may also come inbound, but only if necessary. They should do so only if they have the free time.

DECISION MAKERS AND INFLUENCERS

The funnel's next breakpoint involves the people at A and B accounts who are in the evaluation or decision-making process related to your product or service. This breakpoint is significant because it requires gathering contact information for those people. This is difficult because it usually involves the manual process of looking up the target account and finding the appropriate person at the account, then targeting them with an appropriate message.

There are tools to help do this, on the Tenbound Market Map. These tools can help you identify target accounts in the A through D range, and then, access their data sets to search for the people who are critical to the decision-making process for your product.

Although no data set is perfect, having your team do this research is a huge bonus.

If your team does not have access to a tool, the SDRs (or a research team supporting the SDR team) must do some research on their own.

The manual process of looking people up causes a slowdown, or breakpoint in the funnel, and should be monitored closely in order to alleviate this bottleneck as quickly as possible.

SPEEDING UP THE PROCESS FOR YOUR SDRS

Once you have established who the relevant people (personas) at the target companies are, it is vital to enter that information into a simple, organized database, one that's easy for the SDR to use. Irrelevant or unstructured information only creates more of a bottleneck.

THE TENBOUND DATA CLEANSING PRIORITIZATION FRAMEWORK

tenbound.com

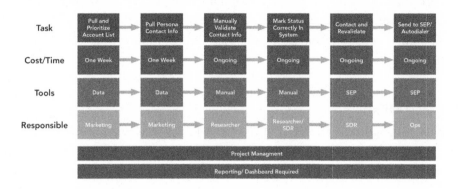

Task	Pull and Prioritize Account List	Pull Persona Contact Info	Manually Validate Contact Info	Mark Status Correctly In System	Contact and Revalidate	Send to SEP/ Autodialer
Cost/Time	One Week	One Week	Ongoing	Ongoing	Ongoing	Ongoing
Tools	Data	Data	Manual	Manual	SEP	SEP
Responsible	Marketing	Marketing	Researcher	Researcher/ SDR	SDR	Ops

Project Managment

Reporting/ Dashboard Required

PERSONA TRAINING

When you have a clear understanding of the personas that your team will be targeting, it is crucial that you train new SDRs. Without a solid understanding of "who" is involved in the influence and decision-making process at your target companies (as it relates to your product or service), it is nearly impossible to engage those targets in a conversation that leads to an appointment. Beyond just researching and finding information on these personas, SDRs must be equipped to engage them in meaningful conversations and convert those to appointments.

We always recommend starting with persona training, only then moving on to product training. This way can we ensure that every SDR can have quality conversations and move the prospect to the next step in the funnel. If SDRs cannot articulate the specific pain points of their prospects, it will be difficult to have the type of conversations they need to have to move them to an appointment.

PAIN POINTS

At this point in the TAM funnel, you must identify if they have a pain point or goal that your company supports.

Your team will interact with people through live conversations, email exchanges, social media, and/or during conference attendance. With any of these modalities, there will be conversations to discover their pain points. It's important to synchronize your efforts with the marketing department so that they are aligned with the pain points or goals that your company supports. You want the Marketing team to be on the same page with the Sales Development team.

We're trying to find out if the targeted individual has any of the pain points and/ or goals you support. Specifically, your team must identify if these pain points or goals are important enough to the target to persuade them to move forward and accept a meeting.

COMMITMENT

This brings us to the bottom of the TAM funnel which is commitment. Is the prospect committed enough to take a meeting? Have your Sales Development team's selling skills sufficiently persuaded them to add a meeting on their calendar when you invite them? Do they have enough of a reason to not only press accept on the calendar invite, but to keep it on their calendar a week later?

That is why we always recommend a Sales Development team set meetings on the same day that they engage the persona or at worst the next day.

Never Wait to Set a Meeting Unless It's Absolutely Necessary.

Low commitment means that the prospect will find themselves looking at their calendar and debating if they still want to meet. If they are not completely committed, they will simply delete the calendar invite with little or no explanation.

We've seen Sales Development teams get strung along for months by the perfect persona of an account, who stated that they had a pain point. Without getting the prospect "bought-in," you miss the critical part of the TAM funnel—commitment to taking the appointment. If the prospect is nice, they will reschedule. They may push the appointment out a week or, unfortunately, forget about it entirely. In the worst-case scenario, the appointment never takes place.

IN SUMMARY

The TAM funnel aligns executives in Marketing, Sales Development, and Sales around pushing your efforts in a synchronized way to:

IDENTIFY

✓ The target accounts at the top of the funnel

✓ The personas that are involved in the decision-making of your product

✓ The pain points and the goals of the prospect so that the messaging resonates

✓ Gain prospect commitment

✓ Take the appointment

If everyone is aligned on these points, it becomes a machine and the choke points that exist can be attacked in a unified manner with a unified budget and unified goals.

When synchronized activities take the TAM funnel clarifies what the ultimate ideals are for everyone. This allows us to drive appointments, pipeline, and revenue.

SYNCHRONIZE

This allows us to track critical breakpoints that we have broken down from a mathematical equation. It helps us push prospects down the funnel so we can ask:

✓ Do we have enough accounts?

✓ Do we have enough A and B accounts? Are they identified correctly?

✓ Does everyone have access to the personas?

✓ Do we have a good idea about who the buyer is?

✓ Do we have the data on the personas and is it organized in a way that's helpful and easy for the Sales Development reps?

✓ Do we need help with the research?

✓ Are the Sales Development reps trained enough to talk to the personas?

✓ Have they had enough coaching and development to truly drive the commitments on the appointments?

Those questions are critical to the Sales Development Leaders. The answers should guide your priorities.

TAKEAWAYS

✓ Determine what percentage of revenue is expected from your team.

✓ Study the creation of a pipeline and determine how much needs to be produced to hit your revenue goal.

✓ If your goal is realistic, break down the steps needed to achieve it.

✓ Use outsourced lead generation, if necessary, to augment the internal team's efforts.

✓ Make sure you are tracking relevant metrics.

✓ Understand your total addressable market.

RESULTS

As the leader of the Sales Development function at your company, driving results is your most critical role.

The further up the food chain you go as a leader, the more the conversations change from people and process to numbers. Team dynamics and complexities are no longer the main topics of conversation; instead, it's all about the numbers—conversion rates, results, and ROI of the Sales Development function.

You should never stray from thinking about people and process, but it's definitely never too early in your career to start thinking about the numbers.

Numbers are the language of business and if you want to move up within a company, you have to be able to communicate in that language.

Part of your job is to optimize performance in the most effective way, which leads to a return on investment for the business you're in. Your team must be making money for the company, and you must be able to monitor and report on this.

In the previous chapter, we discussed the metrics you should be tracking. In this chapter, we dive deeper into the topic of what you should be monitoring and how to achieve better reporting.

■ WHAT YOU SHOULD BE MONITORING

The Sales Development teams' main job is to forge relationships with potential customers. Your team must be highly effective at having conversations, which lead to sales appointments and ultimately, revenue.

Conversations can take place on any available channel, whether it be over the phone, live events, video, email, social media, or chat. There are even channels that we have not even invented yet.

If holograms become an acceptable form of communication, by all means, ensure your team is trained on how to use them, and you have metrics set up to track their performance.

Kudos to the SDR who figures out how to order qualified appointments on an Amazon Echo speaker.

As the leader of the Sales Development team, it is your role to facilitate the process of forging those conversations. In setting up your metrics, you want to understand how those conversations are taking place and how they are converting to qualified appointments.

Let's discuss monitoring conversations across phone, email, and social.

PHONE

The phone may be the most powerful tool in your Sales Development arsenal. The phone is immediate, it's human. You can pick up the nuances of conversation quickly. When you get a person live on the phone, you win fast or lose them just as quickly.

A telephone connect is the fastest way to communicate with prospects, without seeing them live face-to-face. At the same time, the phone is getting harder and harder to use as a breakthrough prospecting tool, because answer rates are lower. A lot of this is due to the advent of power dialers, robocalls, and automatic voice drops.

There is a hot debate found on social media about cold calling.

On one side, sales gurus will say that cold calling is dead. On the other hand, some will argue cold calling works and you should be doing it all day. The real answer lies somewhere in between. While the phone remains the fastest and most customizable communication channel we have available now, it's also getting harder and more time consuming to actually get a prospect on the phone. Whole companies exist only to dial the phone and make connections for your SDRs, so they don't have to spend their time doing it.

THE BOTTOM LINE:

✓ Try different communication channels

✓ Measure what is working and what is not

✓ Double down on the channel that is working best.

MEASURING PHONE EFFECTIVENESS

Measuring the results and effectiveness of your team's phone efforts is essential. It starts with activity. You should hold each member of your team accountable for a specific number of calls per day.

To measure the effectiveness of your phone outreach, simply look at the results.

HOW MANY CONVERSATIONS ARE TAKING PLACE EACH DAY WITH QUALIFIED PROSPECTS IN YOUR IDEAL CUSTOMER PROFILE?

We call these "connects."

HOW LONG ARE THOSE CONVERSATIONS?

We call this "talk time."

HOW MANY OF THESE CONVERSATIONS RESULT IN APPOINTMENTS?

We call this percentage "conversion."

Once you are tracking all these numbers, you can begin to assess the phone effectiveness of your team. If conversations are not converting to appointments, there's a problem with the quality of the conversations that are taking place.

✓ If calls made aren't leading to connections, there's a problem with the list that your team is calling.
✓ If talk time is low, your reps need help keeping prospects on the phone.

Tracking all this data is great, but if you never use it to improve your team's effectiveness...

It becomes pointless.

Don't let your team's hard work go to waste because they don't have the necessary skills to be successful on the phone.

Here are four example scenarios to help illustrate what plays out in the real world.

SCENARIO 1:

If you're seeing that a healthy amount of the dials your team is making are leading to conversations that become appointments, consider your team in good phone shape Keep up the good work.

SCENARIO 2:

If your team is making a lot of dials but convert to few conversations with very few appointments, then there may be something wrong with your phone data and/or your team effectiveness.

Outsourced data providers can help you clean your data, find the right people, and make lists. Agent-assisted dialers can help your team make more calls in less time. Finally, more phone training can help your team improve their skills.

SCENARIO 3:

If you see a low number of dials that lead to a robust number of conversations, and a good trend line of appointments being set, your data is good, your team is well trained and now you just need to increase the number of dials or scale up your team. Add fuel to the fire.

SCENARIO 4:

Does your reporting indicate the SDRs are making a connection but are not able to set appointments? Several tools on the market can help clarify the quality of the conversations that are taking place on calls. Check the Conversational Intelligence section on the Tenbound Market Map.

If the conversation does not last five to 10 seconds, something is not resonating with the prospect. This could be a training issue, or something wrong with the script or with the data that's been provided. Maybe your message is not resonating with people because they don't have a pain point that you could potentially solve.

EMAIL

Busy executives live in their email boxes. Email from work can be loaded onto personal phones and they are constantly checking messages. As they get busier, email begins to represent two major inputs: Either something that is going to make them money or something that's going to get them in trouble.

As they go further up the chain this could mean various things, but it can basically be broken down into those two buckets. Everything else becomes noise.

WILL THIS MAKE ME MONEY?

When a busy executive gets an email, they scan it quickly to understand if it's something that needs to be addressed or that can help them in some way.

- ✓ Will it help them fix a business problem that they have?
- ✓ Will it fix a problem they're having in their upward relationships?
- ✓ Will it help increase their personal income?
- ✓ Will it help them run their team more effectively and more efficiently?

An email that helps with the above issues could be the main impetus for getting the prospect to respond. Take a look at the emails being sent out from your team. Do they fall into this bucket?

Executives who get hundreds of emails every day may have difficulty deciding which are important. It is, therefore, vital to keep the emails short, to the point, and focused on solving one of their business issues.

WILL THIS GET ME IN TROUBLE?

Another hot button with executives as they scan their email box is figuring out if this email will get them in trouble somehow.

✓ Am I late with something?

✓ Is my boss upset?

✓ Is the board upset?

✓ Are the numbers not good?

✓ Is my partner mad at me?

✓ Do I owe money (taxes, late fees, etc.)?

A variety of different things could potentially get an executive in trouble. Just as our ancestors scanned the savanna for signs of danger, human beings and executives are also scanning their inboxes for signs of peril.

The media feeds on this by splashing horrible headlines, so we click on them. It works.

It is important to be vigilant in inspecting what your team is sending to prospects. Read their emails often and ensure they are using proper grammar, spelling and punctuation. You are responsible for the team's performance, and you would never want to find out too late in the game, that your team is damaging your company brand through poorly written emails.

Now that we've got a basic understanding of why executives might open or reply to your email, how do we use that understanding to start and maintain a conversation that leads to a sales appointment?

WHEN IT COMES TO EMAILS, WE'RE LOOKING FOR THE "VOLLEY RESPONSE" (SEE CHAPTER 5).

HOW TO ENCOURAGE VOLLEY RESPONSES

To set your system up to encourage a volley, track assiduously how many volleys are happening on a daily, weekly, monthly and quarterly basis. Volleys are what you're looking for, and what you truly need to focus on throughout this process.

If you look at your reports and you see you are seeing a lot of emails being sent out, but there is a low number being replied to, it could be a messaging problem. Does your email have a strong enough call-to-action? Are you getting a high amount of volleys but without many meetings? Check how those conversations are going and make sure they are driving towards a meeting.

LEVERAGING SOCIAL MEDIA

There is a lot of uncertainty and confusion right now in the Sales Development community about how to best use social media. These channels can be a fantastic way to start conversations (two volleys) on the social platforms. Using in-app messaging and videos are a great way to make connections.

The same rules for email hold for social media. Make the messaging about gain or pain, but never spam people on social media. Your team will be blocked. Spam on social media is the same as the spam you get in email…

irrelevant, untargeted messages that clog up your inbox.

As we all know, social media can also be a huge time waster if not used correctly. Be sure your team can balance the immense potential of social media without getting sucked down the rabbit hole of wasted time and endless scrolling.

For most B2B organizations, LinkedIn is the probably the most relevant Social Media platform. Let's discuss how to leverage LinkedIn.

LINKEDIN

There is a classic debate about LinkedIn that we will not try and squash. Should you be actively selling on LinkedIn or should you be engaging directly with prospective customers?

LinkedIn is a resource for people to gain information, join groups, network with professionals and look for new job opportunities. The people on LinkedIn don't necessarily go there looking for a sales pitch from one of your SDRs.

SDRs should use Linkedin as a place to learn from and interact with their prospective community, support their activities, and connect in a way where they can add value with quality content both created and shared. They should stay away from the "connect and pitch", where you simply connect with people in order to immediately pitch them on your product.

LinkedIn is a great way to grab the attention of your buyer and engage them in conversation. It is not a great place to pitch your solution. The ladder[i] is a strategy that is running rampant and it can generate some short-term results, but it's short-sighted. Here's why. In the world of B2B sales timing is everything.

There are multiple estimates that say only 3% of your target market is ready to buy now[ii]. So, what does that mean? If your team messages a pitch to a prospect, 97% of the time they won't be ready. And guess what happens when they reach out again? The prospect won't be ready. And again?

What results is a LinkedIn inbox that's a graveyard of unsuccessful, automated, thoughtless pitches.

Here is a simple 4 step framework for your team when using LinkedIn for prospecting.

1. Create content regularly about the industry you're selling to.
2. Get your co-workers to like/comment as soon as your team members make a post (the LinkedIn algorithm likes this).
3. Engage with people in the industry you serve through comments.
4. Direct message potential customers to spark a conversation, not a sales pitch.

For the above framework to be successful it requires your reps to build an audience that's both relevant and engaged. Those two things are typically related. The more relevant your content is the more engaged your audience will be. Engagement is important because that's how you get visibility. The more engaged the audience is, the more LinkedIn will show your content to other users. However, there is one problem.

Many times, the person who is responsible for deciding to purchase your solution is not highly engaged on LinkedIn. They may lurk from time to time but that doesn't help you as much as if they engaged with your content via comments and reactions.

---

i   Thomas Grubert, Laddering: A Technique to Find Out What People Value, B2B International, *A ladder is a tool designed to allow you to reach something otherwise unreachable. In the same way, "laddering" as applied to structured questioning is a technique designed to acquire nuggets of information which are otherwise very difficult to get at.* https://www.b2binternational.com/publications/laddering-technique-find-what-people-value/, nd, np.

ii   One such reference is Chet Holmes, *The Ultimate Sales Machine: Turbocharge Your Business with Relentless Focus on 1*, Portfolio, 2007.

HOW DO YOU SOLVE THIS PROBLEM?

Have your team build an audience of both decision-makers and end-users.

As an example, let's say you sell a marketing automation tool to Chief Marketing Officers. Here is exactly how we suggest you would use LinkedIn.

✓ 80% of connection requests are to Marketing Managers

✓ 20% of connection requests are to CMOs.

HOW TO MAKE THE CONNECTION

✓ Write posts and create videos that provide value to Marketing Managers.

✓ Engage with Marketing Managers via comments and DMs (direct messages) without any sales intent.

✓ Message the CMO with the intent to engage in a conversation and validate a need.

If there is a need…

Book that meeting.

Ultimately the goal is still to generate volleys. Since it is difficult to track volleys on Linkedin, you may need to have your SDRs do self-reporting in order to see what's working and what's not. Without getting overly technical, simply have them bring you volleys that meet the one-on-one requirement, so that they bring you the two volleys they've created during the week. Have your team bring you their volleys to review in your 1 on 1's.

This may seem a bit machine-like, but once you understand the volume of activity, you can drill down on the quality.

If you have no understanding of the volume of activity, then it is difficult to understand the quality of the same.

What is measured is improved.

ACHIEVE BETTER REPORTING

Sometimes, you just simply need better reporting. Without strong reporting you will not be able to answer questions like "will an outsourced team help me accelerate our efforts?" or "do I need to increase the activity levels of my team to deliver stronger results?"

You have to analyze data constantly and ask yourself questions on how to improve. Then, you must report back to your boss on what you're finding and what you're doing to improve the efforts of your team.

The true value of metrics is identifying what needs to improve and the impact of making that improvement. That's why it's so important that you have within your own skill set, a strong analytical ability. If you don't have that ability, consider hiring an analyst to sit at your side and help you crunch the numbers in order to make data-driven decisions. Alternatively, if you have the time, learn it yourself.

IDENTIFYING CHOKE POINTS

While no one expects you to become a sales-operations professional, there are major advantages to understanding how to set up your own reporting, even at a basic level. You should know how to create a dashboard for tracking data-driven decisions.

Looking back on the funnel choke point, you should be able to monitor the key performance indicators for each bottleneck and understand where you need to make improvements.

FINDING SUPPORT

Get support in this endeavor either within your own company or online, through resources that you can tap into through online communities. Your dashboard should have a basic green, yellow and red for each key performance indicator, auto refreshed and emailed out to all the stakeholders every day, at a minimum. It may be difficult to set this up at first, but do not stop until you get what you need from reporting. Don't give up until you get the data you want/need.

There are two business books that we recommend highly: Eliyahu Goldratt's, *The Goal: A Process of Ongoing Improvement*[iii] and Justin Roff-Marsh's *The Machine: A Radical Approach to the Design of the Sales Function*[iv].

---

iii   Eliyahu Goldratt, *The Goal: A Process of Ongoing Improvement*, 3rd Edition, North River Press, 2012
iv   Justin Roff-Marsh's *The Machine: A Radical Approach to the Design of the Sales Function*, Independently published, 2013

FROM GOLDRATT

In Goldratt's book, he explains you have to understand your process chokepoints in order to ensure that you have control of them and can improve performance.

Usual choke points include:

- ✓ Dials to appointments conversion rate
- ✓ Appointments to pipeline conversion rate
- ✓ Pipeline to deals closed won conversion rate

Other metrics to watch:

- ✓ Attrition rate for your team
- ✓ Email response rates

FROM ROFF-MARSH

In Roff-Marsh's book, he looks at what goes into engineering the sales machine process. By mapping and diagramming the sales process and applying continuous improvement procedures, Sales Development Leader can drive sustained improvement and efficiency using constant iteration. This compares to applying science to an artform.

THE WHITEBOARD APPROACH

You can easily graph your process with it. If you need a place to start, use two or three of your top-performing SDRs to help you map it out on a whiteboard.

From the whiteboard, transfer the image to an online charting tool and you will begin to understand where there might be gaps in the process.

These gaps are black holes that suck up
opportunities to make money.

The prospecting funnel must include the activities, the conversion rate per activity, and time productivity. Each of these inputs can be a bottleneck for which you will need to increase the velocity.

TAKEAWAYS

✓ Keep your eye on the results from phone, email, and social media.

✓ Use volleys as a baseline to help understand the effectiveness of written communication.

✓ Track everything, even if you have to do it manually.

✓ Outline your process to identify choke points and come up with solutions.

✓ Get very good at analyzing data.

REPUTATION

If you have made it this far through the book, your Sales Development program should be humming along, like a well-oiled machine with a clear strategy, flawless tactical planning, and the right people involved. You should also have reporting and metrics in place to help manage your program on a daily, weekly, and monthly basis and, you should be delivering solid results.

Now's the time to think about where your career can go within your organization, the greater Sales Development community, and...

The World.

Within the daily grind of running a high-performance Sales Development program, it is extremely easy to lose sight of the overall plan for your career. After all, you have so much on your plate right now. How can you think beyond the end of this month or quarter?

It is a fair question, and one that's easy to answer. We are not suggesting you focus on your next promotion or map out the rest of your career path, if that was even possible. What we are suggesting is that you engage in behavior that will put you in a position to get the position you want in the future.

Ignoring career development would be a mistake, but one that can be avoided through good habits and a few simple and repeated daily actions. This chapter will help set you up for success throughout your career while you spend most of your energy driving results from your team.

THE INTERNAL AND EXTERNAL REPUTATION

INTERNAL REPUTATION DEFINED

Your internal reputation is how you are perceived within your company. Your internal brand is critical in being able to help you obtain resources, open doors to new opportunities and move up the chain of command. It's important to promote your success within the company and promote the success of your team members as they move up through the company.

EXTERNAL REPUTATION DEFINED

External reputation is your personal brand image in the marketplace. With the advent of Linkedin, your resume is online, and your achievements are visible for everyone to see. Are you presenting yourself as a recognized thought leader in your industry? Does your profile adequately reflect your achievements? In today's competitive marketplace, you must take ownership of how you are perceived.

MANAGING YOUR INTERNAL REPUTATION

Your internal reputation has a huge impact on your career. The challenge is that this impact is often invisible, taking place in closed-door meetings and social gatherings. As you move up the corporate ladder, there becomes more of a blending between departments. The VP of Sales and the Head of Product Development might be close friends, even if the SDR and Product teams rarely get together.

How everyone in the company perceives you is impacted by social dynamics. This is why managing your internal reputation requires focus on two key relationships—the relationship you have with your direct supervisor, and the relationship you have with other departments.

RELATIONSHIP WITH YOUR SUPERVISOR

When we ask Sales Development Leaders especially newer ones, about their most important relationship in the company, their first response is "my team" or "the prospects."

Of course, it is important to support your team in a positive way and to be sure they have everything they need to be successful and, of course, your prospects are also critical to your success.

The most important relationship you have at your company is with your immediate supervisor, which is often overlooked.

If your boss is supportive, transparent and a decent human being, you are fortunate in the corporate world. Such a boss gives you the assurance that you have a future in the company and will empower you to be successful.

Your boss has a tremendous amount of power over your ability to set up your team for success and to execute the plan you have developed. Your boss can also be a huge advocate for you behind the scenes, to acquire the time and resources that you need, to execute your plan quicker and more efficiently.

People struggle with the concept of promoting themselves to their boss because they don't want to be considered obsequious.

TEAM PROMOTION

How do you promote your success in a way that doesn't seem like you're desperate for a pat on the back?

VERBAL PROMOTION

The best way to do this is by verbally promoting the people on your team. Talk about the success of your team, individually and collectively. Promote the results the team gets and highlight what is driving those results. Don't be shy about reporting that an SDR is doing a great job and when you do, make sure it's backed up with what you have done enhance the processes.

For example, "The SDR team covering the Western region had been surpassing quota by 10% for the past 2 quarters." Providing concrete and concise numbers to your supervisor that you're on top of what's happening on your team.

The effectiveness of your team reflects on you as a leader and communicating that effectiveness to your boss is a perfect way to show that they can trust you to keep everything under control. This positively reflects on you as a leader.

IMPROVING A POOR RELATIONSHIP WITH YOUR BOSS

In a perfect world, you have a great relationship with your boss and everything is sunshine and rainbows. Unfortunately, your relationship with your boss can also go the opposite way. Outside of generating results, this can be challenging to improve.

Here are some tips for improving your relationship with your boss:

- ✓ Make your priorities clear and aligned with results
- ✓ Consistently ask for honest feedback
- ✓ Get to know them outside of working hours
- ✓ Treat them like they are your mentor
- ✓ Understand their expectations and show them that you are working to exceed them

LEARNING EXPERIENCE TYPES

LEARNING ONE: TRUST YOUR GUT

If you have set up your program for high performance following the framework you learned here, you are way ahead of most of the other Sales Development Leaders out there.

Sales Development is a young field and it changes every day. Keeping up with all the changes in technology, processes, the key people, and go-to-market strategy requires market skill and aptitude.

If you feel that you are putting together a high-performance program and you are pushing as hard as you can to get results from the program...

Trust Your Gut.

You are closer to the ground and with more context than anyone else in the organization. If you feel something is wrong, and you're not getting the answers you need...

Listen to that feeling...

Your intuition is stronger than you think. If you're feeling the same strong feeling for many days, it's telling you something. Make your plans. You may have allies who can help you clarify the situation and move forward, or you may not. Ultimately, it's up to you how to move forward. It could be worth staying and fighting, or perhaps moving on.

LEARNING TWO: KNOW THE ORGANIZATIONAL STRUCTURE

Diagram the hierarchy of your company officers from your boss and your boss's boss to everyone whose sphere influences you. Map out that structure by drafting a dotted line connecting all the people involved in the go-to-market strategy.

Since you know everyone involved, you must work to build relationships with those people. Take those people out to lunch or set up a video call. Meet up to talk about things outside of work. Something more human or personal. These relationships are essential and will lead to having allies across the organization and will give you visibility into what's going on at a higher level.

LEARNING THREE: STAND UP FOR YOURSELF

When reflecting on both situations I illustrated above, I wish I would have stood up for myself earlier. Before I quit. I had the CEO conversation and could tell he knew nothing about what a psychopath the head of sales actually was. He had no idea what was going on. Management thought that everything was fine and I was doing a good job.

RELATIONSHIP WITH OTHER DEPARTMENTS

Another large part of your internal reputation is how other departments perceive you. After you have mapped out the various departments involved in the go-to-market strategy, get to know the heads of sales, marketing, consumer success, and finance. Build those relationships early and keep them strong throughout your career.

These relationships are important during your time at the company and beyond.

You never know when you will need to make a withdrawal from the "relationship bank" and if you haven't been putting anything in, you're going to be overdrawn.

— Ralph Barsi

Do not miss an opportunity to take coworkers out to lunch, go for coffee, go for a walk, or call a meeting to understand what they are working on and how you can support them. Get to know them personally and professionally, and be as helpful as you can.

One way to be helpful is to identify a few of their major goals and how you could help to achieve those goals. Offer to help when you can and have no strings attached.

Keep in mind that there may be a time you need their help. When that time comes, you don't want it to be the first time you ever said hello.

MANAGING YOUR EXTERNAL REPUTATION

Sometimes called a personal brand, your external reputation is how you are perceived by the marketplace. Typically, there are two components to building a strong external reputation–personal branding and content creation.

PERSONAL BRANDING

Sales Development legend Ralph Barsi stresses, "You always need to be thinking about your brand in the marketplace."[i]

The concept of brand building is misunderstood. Building your brand is not about gaining millions of Instagram followers or posting lots of stuff online. But those activities may be components of branding. A personal brand is an expansion of your resume. It helps you stand out from the crowd and can provide you with more opportunities throughout your career.

You might think building a personal brand is wasting time or an exercise in ego. This is utterly untrue. In the last few years, corporate culture has changed dramatically. People within your network carry a supercomputer in their pocket. People spend a tremendous amount of time on social networks online.

In order to compete, you have to be known and be seen.

There are people out there that can have a huge impact on your career but don't know you yet. Those people have no idea of your capacity to get things done or what your level of expertise is.

People you may need for your career don't know you and so they don't yet know your capacity to get things done. They may want to hire you, recommend you or refer you. When they see you online, it's important that they know exactly how you can help them. So how do you go about building a personal brand?

i   *https://ralphbarsi.com/*

■ BUILDING YOUR BRAND

CORE REQUIREMENTS FOR BUILDING AN EFFECTIVE PERSONAL BRAND

Here are the three core things you must do to effectively build a personal brand.

1: HAVE A GOAL

Decide what metrics you are tracking and make sure you are keeping your eye on it. We recommend using a ratio of likes/comments to views as your goal. This metric is good because it is calculating how many people actually engage with your post based on how many people viewed it. Sometimes posts don't get adequate visibility, but they do get high amounts of engagement. Divide the number of likes and comments (removing your own) by the number of total views. A 2% - 3% engagement rate is strong[ii].

2: CHOOSE AN INDUSTRY

When building a personal brand, it is important you choose which industry you want to have that reputation in. If you don't select an industry you will be posting content that is general and less valuable. By not having an industry focus you are also missing out on showing your industry expertise. Having a reputation as an industry expert is where you will receive a lot of career benefits from having a strong personal brand.

3: PROVIDE VALUE

The third and most challenging is providing value to the audience you are building within a specific industry. This value is realized by posting content, engaging in discussions, and sharing other meaningful content. This is how you will stand out and build that reputation. It requires commitment. You must create content regularly.

---

ii   Sales Success Stories Podcast, Scott Ingram research, *https://top1.fm/about/*

CREATING CONTENT

Growing an audience comes from creating valuable content and distributing it. We break content up into three categories.

1. Blog Posts
2. Social Posts
3. Newsletters/podcasts

Make it a habit to regularly write a blog and post on social media. Having a newsletter or podcast can also have a huge impact, but we understand that not everyone has the time after work hours for these more challenging content types.

BLOG POSTS

We would encourage you to create your own blog. Having a LinkedIn page and other social media is great, but the next step is to have your own blog website that describes who you are as a person beyond the constraints of a social media page.

You can create a website with your own domain name for less than $100 a year. A small investment to be able to control how you are perceived and consolidate your content across all social channels.

CONTENT IDEAS

The first step to creating valuable content for your audience is to list out major problems within the industry. Go into detail on each challenge and identify where are people getting stuck, if there are any gaps, and what the difficulties are.

By outlining these challenges and the specific details that make them up, you have the start of your content plan.

COMMON PROBLEMS IN THE SALES DEVELOPMENT WORLD

✓ Cold calling difficulties

✓ High SDR attrition

✓ High SDR burn out

✓ Low results (ROI) on program

✓ Poor data integration leading to inefficiency

COMMON PROBLEMS IN THE CYBERSECURITY WORLD

✓ Poor user behavior

✓ Constantly changing attacker strategies

✓ Lack of transparency in systems

✓ Overlapping vendor solutions

Each of these problems can be content you explore and help with.

EXAMPLE:

Here is an example if we were to focus on one SDR challenge.

✓ Challenge: Cold calling is hard for SDRs

✓ How to ace a cold call introduction

✓ Overcoming common objections

✓ How to speak with confidence on a cold call

✓ How long should you wait before cold calling someone again

✓ Cold calling techniques

✓ Cold call script

As you can see, there is a lot you can do within just one challenge.

Once you have all the common challenges outlined and some related topics to discuss, it is time to actually make the content. Here are some ideas.

✓ Whiteboard video series that you post on YouTube and your blog.

✓ Write detailed articles about how to solve specific challenges or improve a skill.

✓ Do a mini blog series giving tactical advice to solve large challenges.

✓ Q&A articles or videos where you answer questions from audience members.

✓ Interview articles or videos where you interview industry experts.

✓ Hire a researcher to put together some industry research papers together for you.

There is no shortage of ideas, you just need to choose what aligns with your skill set and get started.

We suggest sticking to one social media platform to begin with. The most obvious is LinkedIn, but go with any platform where your audience is active and where you will make a commitment.

TIME ALLOCATION FOR CONTENT

You should be spending an hour or two on this a week. Keep your time allocation consistent. It may take a long time to become habit, but it will be worth the effort.

It's hard to quantify the return on this investment but the power of social media is amazing. You never know who you will attract by creating and maintaining your online presence.

THE IMPORTANCE OF BRANDING

Branding is no longer just a nice option or an exercise in ego. You must think of it as career insurance for the coming years. We know many productive and talented SDR leaders who have no online presence. If they change their jobs or are laid off, they may be left sailing upstream without an oar.

New clients, prospective employers, and potential employees must be able to find and learn about you online before making a commitment.

Right now, what will they find?

✓ Do you have any how-to videos?

✓ Have you reviewed or commented on any posts?

✓ Have you spoken at any conferences recently?

✓ Have you been on any podcasts?

Positive value in the marketplace depends
on contributions like these.

Reputation is shaped by results.

At the end of the day, you can have the best external branding and the best internal relationships, but if you don't generate results, it's all for naught.

In this chapter we discussed how to manage your internal and external reputation. This is an important skill but there is something we don't want to ever forget.

Results are ALWAYS the main priority.

As a leader you must control what you can control and empower your team members to do the same. There is no amount of personal branding that will make up for a bad reputation.

Put results first and the optics second. Just don't neglect to build strong relationships and provide value to your audience.

TAKEAWAYS

✓ Build your reputation within your company by establishing friendly relationships with those above you and with your colleagues and delivering consistent results.

✓ Your boss must know not only of your accomplishments but those of your team as well.

✓ Build your reputation online through personal branding and content creation.

✓ Devote at least an hour or two a week to content personal branding and content.

THE SALES DEVELOPMENT FRAMEWORK—CONCLUSION

Now you have the tools needed to build a world class Sales Development program and must execute.

Start with your culture and understand how it fits into your leadership style. Understand the difference between Leadership and Management, and always use your determined leadership style in your recruiting, hiring, and onboarding philosophy. Write your One Page Summary and put a note on your calendar to revisit it once a quarter. Never sacrifice culture because you are desperate or pressured to hire.

Remember to emphasize training for your team each week, and back it up with continuous and ongoing coaching. Do not treat training and coaching like a pesky weekly task you have to complete. The investment you make in your team will yield stronger results more than anything else.

Soon, you will see the results of your efforts, whether good or bad. Analyze them and use that data to push your program forward or, when necessary, make course corrections. As you keep pushing your team forward with data driven leadership, you will start to see better results. Take those results and inspire your team to build on that momentum. Shout your success from the rooftops to build your team's reputation and your professional brand in the marketplace.

At that point your personal brand will be raised and the culture that you want to create will continue to perpetuate throughout the rest of your career, continuously improving and mirroring your career success.

Remember, highly skilled Sales Development leaders are very rare, so if you can nail this function, the sky's the limit for your career. You shouldn't be just doing it for you. Do it for all the SDRs who are early in their career and need the guidance and support from someone more experienced than them.

Throughout this journey don't lose touch with the community. Build relationships with other SDR leaders and keep in touch with us at tenbound.com and vouris.com, let us know how things are going.

We're excited to join you on this journey towards Sales Development excellence! We have no doubt that you will do some amazing things.

MOVING FORWARD

We trust that now with your great results and stellar reputation you can continue to build an amazing culture and start the entire process over again whether at your current company, a new company, or your own venture.

Although many consider it the hardest job on the go-to-market team, Sales Development can be extremely rewarding and the mastery of skills and abilities to run a high-performance Sales Development program are extremely rare. We all know the theory of supply and demand. By reading this book and practicing the takeaways in each chapter, your skills will increase, demand will increase, and you'll be able to command higher remuneration for your efforts.

Here's to your success.

✵ ✵ ✵

Looking forward to hearing your story.

SINCERELY,

David Dulany

DAVID DULANY, CEO
TENBOUND

Kyle V.

KYLE VAMVOURIS, CEO
VOURIS

SALES DEVELOPMENT TOOLS
& SERVICE QUADRANTS

In the world of Sales Development, there are tools and services for everything. They all have the same purpose— to make Sales Development Representatives more productive and efficient. The goal of this chapter is to give you context on the type of solutions that exist and which of those tools will be helpful when you must search for ways to solve specific problems.

Keeping up with these helpful technology innovations is a full-time job.

CAVEATS: NEW DEVELOPMENTS

There's one obvious challenge when discussing technology and services in a printed book—tools and solution providers are constantly changing, so we're including a chapter that discusses the different categories (or quadrants) within the world of Sales Development technology and services.

Bookmark the tenbound.com Market Map for the latest advances in Sales Development Tools & Services.

ACCOUNT-BASED MARKETING

Technology in this category is designed to help organize data and provide intelligence when working with account-focused strategies. If your reps struggle organizing leads within your CRM, based on what company they work for, this is what you are looking for.

EXAMPLE:

If your company is targeting accounts in the oil & gas industry, the Account Based Marketing program will list accounts in that industry, and then target people at those companies with specific advertising, then show you if anyone at those targeted companies have engaged with your materials. This is great information for the SDRs because they can be sure they're targeting the right accounts and engaging with people at those companies who have interacted with their advertisements.

Account Based software programs allow managers to help prioritize at the account level, target those accounts with specific advertising, and drive account specific campaigns for SDRs to focus on.

API CONNECTORS

API connectors are tools that allow you to automate actions between two applications that do not integrate. For example, you use Software A and Software B and they do not talk to each other. If you want something to happen in Software A when a record in Software B is updated, you will need an API connector.

AUTO DIALERS/SALES ACCELERATION

This technology is designed to help salespeople do more activities in less time. From automatically dialing lead after lead to dialing multiple leads at once and connecting you to whoever answers, these tools accelerate sales activity.

AUTOMATED LEAD MANAGEMENT

Automated Lead Management companies develop AI assistants who communicate in a human-like manner, with leads, prospects, customers, employees, and other persons of interest, via webchat, email, and text. The bots leverage natural language understanding, natural language processing, natural language generation, deep learning, and machine learning, to convert interest to qualified leads.

CALENDAR

Calendar tools allow reps to schedule meetings through a tool instead of needing to look between multiple calendars to find the best time. In addition, these tools allow prospects to schedule directly by clicking a calendar link.

COMMUNITIES

Sales Development communities exist online, in-person, or as a hybrid, in order to help professionals connect, share ideas, work through issues, and support each other in a safe environment. Most communities are free and supported through sponsorships, or are directed to support certain tools and services, i.e. User Groups.

COMPLIANCE

A privacy management platform's mission is to streamline compliance with CASL[i] CCPA[ii], GDPR[iii], and other emerging regulations. These platforms eliminate complicated, manual, and time-consuming processes, making it easier to ensure compliance with those laws.

CONVERSATION INTELLIGENCE

Conversation intelligence tools monitor sales and prospecting calls and provide detailed insights. If you are looking for a way to better coach reps based on call recordings, conversation intelligence tools are for you.

CONVERSATIONAL MARKETING

This category of technology is for tools that allow you to have live conversations with prospects as they engage with your website. Typically, your marketing team would install an online chat tool on the website and your reps would chat with prospects who have questions.

---

i   Canada Anti-Spam Law

ii   California Consumer Privacy Act

iii   General Data Protection Regulation

CRM

Customer Relationship Management software allows you to manage all your leads, deals, and customers in one place. Having a CRM system is common in today's modern business environment.

DATA AND DATA ENRICHMENT

Data is the life blood of Sales Development. Data providers give your team contact information for potential customers. This is necessary if you have an outbound prospecting strategy.

DATA COMPLIANCE

With the many government regulations around data, such as GDPR, CASL and CCPA, a new group of tools has been developed to help Sales Development teams remain in compliance. These are usually managed by a company's executive or legal team.

EMAIL RESPONSE MONITORING

These providers scan your email responses and pull data from them into your CRM. This allows you to mine the responses for the valuable information contained they contain. With plenty of responses coming each day, especially out of office messages, these tools save time and fill your CRM with valuable information.

GAMIFICATION AND MANAGEMENT

Gamification brings in the elements of game playing to reports and dashboards, such as badges and point scoring, and adds a sense of competition and transparency to the daily work of the SDRs. Instead of merely showing backward-looking results, gamified dashboards offer a more interesting and engaging experience for SDRs and that can lead to greater motivation and better results.

This make Sales Development fun while offering Managers a way to monitor and motivate their team by leveraging technology. Dashboards that can flash on desktop and in the office with rotating metrics, charts, and graphs will motivate reps to make more calls, have more conversations and create more pipeline.

LINKEDIN

This is a category all its own, because LinkedIn has a suite of tools that aid in prospecting and sales efforts. If your prospects are on LinkedIn, it is likely worth leveraging the tools they have available.

MAILINGS

This category is for tools that enable your team to send mail directly to their prospects. This could be handwritten notes, swag, and/or gift cards. If direct mail or gift-giving is part of your strategy, these tools are for you.

MARKETING AUTOMATION

Marketing Automation Platforms (aka MAPS) are software programs created for marketing departments and agencies to design multi-channel campaigns, manage them, and automate tasks involved with their execution. Data produced by these systems is then used to improve the results of current and existing marketing efforts.

PRE-HIRING ASSESSMENTS

Using a pre-hiring assessment tool can help you manage high quantities of candidates. These tools can help you narrow your list of candidates down to those that are the most qualified. Assessments are typically helpful if you have a high number of candidates.

RECRUITING

Recruiting tools enable you to manage all of the candidates you are evaluating. These tools are very helpful when you have many applicants and need a way to track where they all are in the process and and will help organize interviews.

REFERRALS

These companies create "warm introductions" by connecting salespeople with their networks and paying them for making those connections. Salespeople upload their contacts and agree to make an introduction for a fee.

SALES ENABLEMENT

A sales enablement platform organizes multiple touchpoints across outreach methods and time. In addition, sales enablement tools help your reps manage, research, and contact prospects. This tool is necessary for you if your reps are using multiple channels as part of their outreach (phone, email, LinkedIn, etc.).

SALES EDUCATION

Training and development programs for students and those professionals at early- and mid-career levels that prepare them for a career in Sales Development. The training can be within a traditional college or university environment, or a private institution that works with employers to instruct new recruits and ensure they perform well when they are hired.

SALES ENGAGEMENT

This is software for Sales Development and Sales teams to organize and automate tasks needed to stay focused and to make certain enough communication with prospects is being performed. It ensures messages are customized, efficient and streamlined. The data produced by these is used to identify which messages, activities, and tactics drive effective sales conversations and increase overall pipeline and sales results.

SIGNATURE MONITORING

These are software tools that give Marketers a centralized dashboard to control and edit the signature blocks of emails being sent out by Sales teams. Information on how the signature is being used by prospects is then displayed on the dashboard and can be used to make editorial decisions on future signatures.

TRAINING AND CONSULTING

These firms work with Sales Development leaders and reps to improve performance through advisory services, training programs, and coaching. They work directly with leaders and reps live, online, or through pre-recorded courses to help teams reach their goals.

VIDEO PROSPECTING

This category is for tools that allow your reps to create one-off video messages and send them to their prospects without the labor typically involved in video production. If you would like your reps to use video as part of their prospecting strategy, this is the best way to do it.

VOIP PHONE

A VOIP Phone system is simply a system that allows you to make phone calls on your computer through the internet. Often this is built into other applications that you may be using but if not, you will need a stand-alone provider.

THE ULTIMATE SALES DEVELOPMENT GLOSSARY

Whether you're new to Sales Development or an experienced pro, Sales Development has its own language; a language that's constantly evolving. To help you out, we've put together a glossary of the most terms used in Sales Development and what you need to know about them.

WHAT IS SALES DEVELOPMENT?
According to Wikipedia, Sales Development is an organization that sits between the marketing and sales functions of a business and is in charge of the front-end of the sales cycle: identifying, connecting with, and qualifying leads[i].

A

ABM – Account-Based Marketing: A growth strategy, where high-value accounts are treated as a 'market of one.' Marketing and sales teams work together to provide selected accounts with a hyper-personalized experience. The SDR role of linking sales and marketing makes them a key component of any successful ABM strategy.

---

i   *https://en.wikipedia.org/wiki/Sales_development*

ACV – Annual Contract Value: The average revenue generated by a contract over a year (excluding any one-off fees, such as setup costs). A metric generally used by SaaS and other subscription-based businesses.

AE – Account Executive: A member of the sales team who focuses on closing deals. In most cases, SDRs will be tasked with delivering SQLs to an Account Executive for them to nurture and close.

AM – Account Manager: A member of the sales team responsible for managing customer accounts that have already closed.

AUTOMATION SOFTWARE: Technology that carries out repetitive tasks on behalf of the user. SDRs can use it to save time by automating mundane low-touch tasks, allowing them to focus on more valuable high-touch activities. Common use cases include dialers and email automation.

B

B2B – Business to Business: A company that predominantly sells products/services to other companies.

B2C – Business to Customer: A company that predominantly sells products/services to individual customers.

BASE SALARY: The fixed amount paid to an employee, excluding any bonuses or commission.

BD – Business Development: Establishing and improving strategic relationships with complementary businesses with the aim of integration and cross-selling.

BDR – Business Development Representative: An alternative title for a Sales Development Representative (SDR). Used by some companies where the role has an increased focus on identifying new markets and making connections with businesses in those markets.

BONUS: An additional payment on top of the employee's base salary to reward performance and meeting/exceeding targets.

BUYER INTENT: Actions or behaviors by an individual/company that indicate they are ready to purchase a specific product/service. For example, SDRs may look for people who are already searching for a similar solution or engaging with sales material.

BUYER PERSONA: A profile that represents your ideal customer, describing the individual and their objectives, pain-points, behaviors, etc. The buyer persona should be based on research and existing customers. SDRs can use this information to tailor their messaging for leads that are a good fit. Different from an ICP, which focuses on the company.

C

CAC – Customer Acquisition Cost: How much it costs a business on average to acquire a new paying customer, taking into account all costs including overheads, salaries, and any additional spend.

CADENCE: Literal meaning is a flow or pattern of events. For SDRs, your cadence will typically refer to the timing of your touchpoints.

CAN-SPAM: A US law governing the sending of commercial emails. SDRs should be familiar with the requirements and ensure that any emails they send are compliant.

CASL: Canada's regulations regarding commercial emails, which prohibits the sending of electronic messages without prior consent and has additional requirements for the contents of any electronic messages.

CCPA: Regulations governing the rights of Californians concerning their data. It only applies to certain businesses, but SDRs should check they're fulfilling their obligations when handling any data that could be potentially linked to a person or household.

CHANNELS: The different methods and means an SDR can use to communicate with leads and prospects, such as email, calls, social media, etc.

CLTV – Customer Lifetime Value: The predicted total revenue that a customer will bring in over the period they remain a customer. For a business to be successful, this should be higher than the customer acquisition cost (CAC).

COLD CALLING: A phone call made to a prospect without any previous engagement or relationship.

COLD EMAILING: An email sent to a prospect without any previous engagement or relationship.

COMMISSION: A payment structure based on results, such as the number of SQLs generated. This is usually in addition to an SDR's base salary.

COMMUNITY (SALES DEVELOPMENT): In-person and online groups of like-minded people solving specific problems related to Sales Development.

CONVERSION: When a prospect takes a desired action, such as responding to an email or agreeing to a meeting. Ultimately, companies will be looking to convert as many prospects into customers as possible.

CRM – Customer Relationship Management: The management of prospect and customer data, including contact information and interactions, usually handled by purpose-built software. SDRs will generally use a CRM to track their outreach and prospect relationships.

C-SUITE: The top-level executives in a business, such as the Chief Executive Officer (CEO), Chief Financial Officer (CFO), and so on. For high-value sales in the B2B environment, a member of the C-Suite may be the decision-maker or otherwise involved in the sales process.

CTA – Call to Action: A sentence requesting the prospect to take a specific action, such as replying to an email, downloading a brochure, or booking a call.

CUSTOMER SUCCESS: A team focused on ensuring the success of existing customers. After the AE closes the deal, the Customer Success team will typically step in to onboard the customer with the aim of increasing customer satisfaction and reducing churn.

D

DEMAND GENERATION: A marketing strategy used to promote awareness of a business and its product/service.

DEMOGRAPHICS: The characteristics of a group, typically based on physical data (such as age, nationality, and sex) and socio-economic information (such as income level, employment, and education level).

DIALER: A piece of software that automates dialing phone numbers.

DIRECT MAIL: The use of physical mail as a sales channel.

E

EMAIL SERVICE PROVIDER: Software used to send, automate, and manage email campaigns.

ENGAGEMENT: Interactions carried out by the prospect with the SDR, measured in terms of action and time (e.g. items downloaded, emails replied to, time spent viewing a presentation).

ENRICHMENT: Expanding on and improving the quality of existing data. For example, an SDR may use contact enrichment to improve the quality of their contact information, uncovering extra details they can use in their outreach.

G

GATEKEEPER: Something (usually a person) who controls access to a person. In Sales Development, this may be a secretary or assistant who answers the phone on behalf of a decision-maker you're trying to reach.

GDPR: The European regulations governing the processing and protection of personal data. For SDRs, this will affect how you gather contact details and how you handle prospect information.

I

ICP – Ideal Customer Profile: A description of the company that is the best fit for your product/service, including details such as their industry, their size, their turnover, and so on. Different from a Buyer Persona, which focuses on the individual buyer.

INBOUND: Prospects that approach your company and express an interest in your product/services, usually as a result of marketing activities.

INSIDE SALES: Sales activities that are carried out from 'inside' the office, such as emails and phone calls, rather than face-to-face interactions.

K

KPI – Key Performance Indicator: The metrics and results used to measure performance and success. For an SDR, a typical KPI might be the number of meetings booked.

L

LDR – Lead Development Representative: An alternative title for a Sales Development Representative (SDR). Usually assigned to following up on inbound leads.

LEAD: A person or business that has the potential to become a customer and has exhibited some form of interest, such as by downloading a whitepaper or requesting additional information.

LEAD GENERATION: Activities carried out by sales/marketing intending to create interest in a product/service and attract leads.

LEAD QUALIFICATION: Determining if a lead is likely to become a customer, typically based on how they compare to the company's ICP.

LEAD SCORING: A method of ranking leads, based on agreed criteria, to determine which leads are most likely to become customers. It can then be used to establish priorities for outreach.

LVR – Lead Velocity Rate: The rate of change of qualified leads, measured monthly.

M

MARGIN: The financial amount gained from a product or service after factoring out selling expenses.

METRICS: The quantifiable results of activities, generally used to determine performance, identify areas for improvement, and predict future results. For example, email outreach metrics would include deliverability, open rate, click-through rate, and reply rate.

MQL – Marketing Qualified Leads: A lead that has demonstrated interest in your product/service, based on their engagement with marketing. An SDR may be handed MQLs for further qualification.

MRR – Monthly Recurring Revenue: The amount of revenue a SaaS or other subscription-based business receives each month, excluding any one-off charges. For customers on an annual payment plan, the annual payment will be represented by monthly payments throughout the year.

O

OKR – Objectives and Key Results: A goal-setting framework businesses use to measure progress by tying objectives to measurable results.

OPTIMIZATION: Improving a process or action so that it's generating the best results. For example, an SDR may modify their call script with the aim of getting more meeting requests.

OUTBOUND: Where an SDR reaches out to potential customers who haven't already displayed any interest in the business's product/service.

OUTSIDE SALES: Sales activities carried out 'outside' the office, interacting with potential customers face-to-face rather than by email or phone.

P

PAIN POINTS: A problem, annoyance, or challenge a prospective customer is facing in their work line.

PERSONA: A generalized set of attributes assigned to prospective and current customers.

PERSONALIZATION: Tailoring messaging or service so that it is specific to the individual, such as by using their name or addressing their unique challenges.

PIPELINE: In sales, a pipeline is used to visualize and track prospects as they move through the different stages of the sales process. It can also be used to describe the number of prospects (or their monetary value) who are currently going through the sales process.

PLAYBOOK: A critical information repository containing everything a Sales Development team needs to be successful.

PROSPECT: A potential customer who has been qualified and is now in the sales process.

PROSPECTING: Reaching out to potential customers and engaging with them, with the objective of creating a sales opportunity.

Q

QUOTA: A sales target given to teams or individuals. Performance against quota is often used to evaluate success and determine any bonus/commission.

R

ROI – Return on Investment: A metric used to determine the profitability of an investment, whether that's time or money. ROI is calculated by deducting the cost of the investment from the gain of the investment, then dividing by the cost of the investment. For example, the ROI of your new CRM might be [$500 (value of time saved) – $100 (cost of software)] divided by [$100 (cost of software)] = 4, a 400% ROI.

S

SAO – Sales Accepted Opportunity: A qualified sales lead.

SALES DEVELOPMENT: The dedicated practice of creating sales pipeline for your company through proactive outreach to prospective customers and following up on inbound leads created by your marketing efforts. Sales Development focuses on the early stages of the sales process, from researching potential prospects to contacting leads and ultimately generating sales-qualified leads (SQLs).

SALES DEVELOPMENT LEADER A sales leader who oversees the Sales Development function in an organization, usually responsible for building and training the Sales Development team.

SALES FUNNEL: A visualization used to track prospects as they move through the sales process, showing how many convert and identifying the drop-off rate at each stage.

SALES TRIGGERS: Any activity or change of circumstances that create a sales opportunity, such as a new investment, change of management, change of location, and so on. By looking out for sales triggers, SDRs can reach out at the right time and personalize their messaging, increasing the chance of a positive response.

SCRAPING: Extracting or 'harvesting' large amounts of data from websites, such as pulling lead contact information from social media sites.

SDR – Sales Development Representative: Salespeople who are responsible for carrying out Sales Development, usually sat between marketing and sales. Their job is to carry out early-stage sales tasks, with the objective of maintaining a full pipeline of qualified leads for the sales team. Once a lead has been qualified, they'll be passed onto an Account Executive.

SEGMENTATION: Breaking down a large market into separate groups that share specific criteria (industry, budget, role, etc.). Proper segmentation allows SDRs to personalize their outreach to each group more effectively.

SOCIAL SELLING: The use of social media as a sales channel. SDRs may use social networks to create valuable content, connect with prospects, and develop stronger business relationships.

SQL – Sales Qualified Lead: A lead that meets the agreed criteria that demonstrate they're more likely to become a customer. Once the SDR qualifies a lead, they'll be passed onto an Account Executives to nurture and close the sale.

T

TEMPLATES: A file or document with the standard information already in place that can then be easily customized. SDRs can use templates with proven frameworks for their email outreach and cold calling scripts to speed up the process and improve results.

TOUCHPOINTS: Points of contact/interaction in the sales process, taking place between a salesperson and a lead. For example, an SDR may use a cadence with ten touchpoints, starting with a cold call, then sending an email, and so on.

U

USP – Unique Selling Point: A statement conveying the unique features that differentiate a company and/or its product from the competition.

V

VALUE PROPOSITION: A statement conveying the results and benefits customers can enjoy as a result of purchasing from a company.

W

WARM OUTREACH: Reaching out to a lead, such as by phone or email, when they're already familiar with the company and there is some level of existing relationship.

Hopefully, this glossary has given you greater clarity on the many terms used in the Sales Development world and answered any questions you might have had. If there are any other terms you've come across that you'd like explained, reach out and let us know; we'll be happy to add them to the list.

RECOMMENDED READING

James Collins, *Good to Great: Why Some Companies Make the Leap and Others Don't*, New York, Harper Business, 2001

Eliyahu Goldratt, *The Goal: A Process of Ongoing Improvement*, 3rd Edition, North River Press, 2012

Darren Hardy, *The Compound Effect: Jumpstart Your Income, Your Life, Your Success*, Hachette Go, 2020

Ashley Kelly, *Scaling a Sales Development Team Fast, and Scaling it Right*, Lever, August 23, 2017,

Steve McClatchy, *Decide: Work Smarter, Reduce Your Stress, and Lead by Example*, Wiley, 2014

David McNally*Be Your Own Brand: Achieve More of What You Want by Being More of Who You Are*, Berrett-Koehler Publishers, 2010

Tim Mooney and Roger O. Brinkerhoff, *Courageous Training: Bold Actions for Business Results*, Berrett-Koehler Publishers, 2008

Jeff Olson and David Mann, *The Slight Edge: Turning Simple Disciplines into Massive Success and Happiness*, Greenleaf Book Group Press, 2013

Darryl Praill, *How to Create a Winning Culture for your Sales Development, Reps,* Vanilla Soft, January 8, 2018

Joe Pulizzi, *Content Inc.: How Entrepreneurs Use Content to Build Massive Audiences and Create Radically Successful Businesses*, McGraw-Hill Education, 2015

Mark Roberge, *The Sales Acceleration Formula*, Wiley, 2015

Justin Roff-Marsh's *The Machine: A Radical Approach to the Design of the Sales Function*, Independently published, 2013

Aaron Ross and Collin Stewart, *Matt Amundson on the core principles of outbound sales*, Predictable Revenue Podcast, 002, May 4, 2017, https://www.youtube.com/watch?v=8HWK9VKNjZw

Kim Scott, *Radical Candor*, New York, St. Martin's Press, 2019

SDR Huddle, *Flip the Funnel: The Science of Onboarding SDRs*, May 10, 2017, https://sdrhuddle.com/2017/05/10/flip-the-funnel-the-science-of-onboarding-sdrs/

Geoff Smart and Randy Street, *WHO, The A Method for Hiring*, Ballantine Books, 2008

Michael D. Watkins and Peter F. Drucker, *HBR's 10 Must Reads for New Managers*, Harvard Business Review, 2019

Jocko Willink and Leif Babin, *Extreme Ownership*, New York, St. Martins Press, 2015, 2017

ABOUT THE AUTHORS

DAVID DULANY

David Dulany is Founder and CEO of Tenbound, a research and advisory firm that's 100% focused and dedicated to Sales Development. Tenbound has become the hub of the Sales Development industry, with a thriving online research center, tech market map, tool directory, training and consulting programs, and The Tenbound Sales Development Conferences. David lives in the San Francisco Bay area with his wife, two kids, and one dog. You can learn about Tenbound at www.tenbound.com

KYLE VAMVOURIS

Kyle Vamvouris is the CEO of Vouris & author of the bestselling sales book, Cold to Committed. Having helped over a thousand SDRs and dozens of startups, Kyle is passionate about early-stage growth and works with startup companies to help them build, scale, and optimize their sales teams. Kyle lives in the San Francisco Bay Area with his wife, two kids, and their two dogs. You can learn about his services or read his articles at www.vouris.com.

INDEX

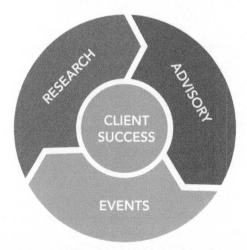